STEVE HAWKE

A TOWN IS BORN

THE FITZROY CROSSING STORY

This is a Magabala Book

LEADING PUBLISHER OF ABORIGINAL AND
TORRES STRAIT ISLANDER STORYTELLERS.

CHANGING THE WORLD, ONE STORY AT A TIME.

Aboriginal and Torres Strait people are advised that this publication contains names and images of deceased persons. Approval has been obtained from the appropriate people to publish these names and images.

First published 2013, reprinted 2014
New ed 2019, reprinted 2021, 2023, 2025
Magabala Books Aboriginal Corporation,
1 Bagot Street, Broome, Western Australia
www.magabala.com email: sales@magabala.com

Magabala Books is assisted by the Australian Government through Creative Australia, its principal arts investment and advisory body. The State of Western Australia has made an investment in this project through the Department of Local Government, Sport and Cultural Industries.

Magabala Books is an independent Aboriginal and Torres Strait Islander publishing house. We acknowledge the Traditional owners of the Country on which we live and work. We recognise and respect the unbroken connections to traditional lands, waters, and cultures. Through what we publish we honour all our Elders, peoples and stories, past, present and into our collective futures.

Cover Design by Jo Hunt
Typeset by Post Pre-press Group
Printed by Griffin Press
9781925936858 (paperback)

This manuscript was developed through the support of Kimberley Aboriginal Law and Cultural Centre (KALACC).

A catalogue record for this book is available from the National Library of Australia

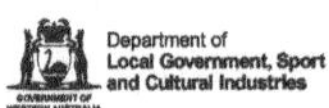

For the men and women who led their communities with vision and courage through the extraordinary upheavals of the 1960s and 70s.

STATION BOUNDARIES PRE-1980

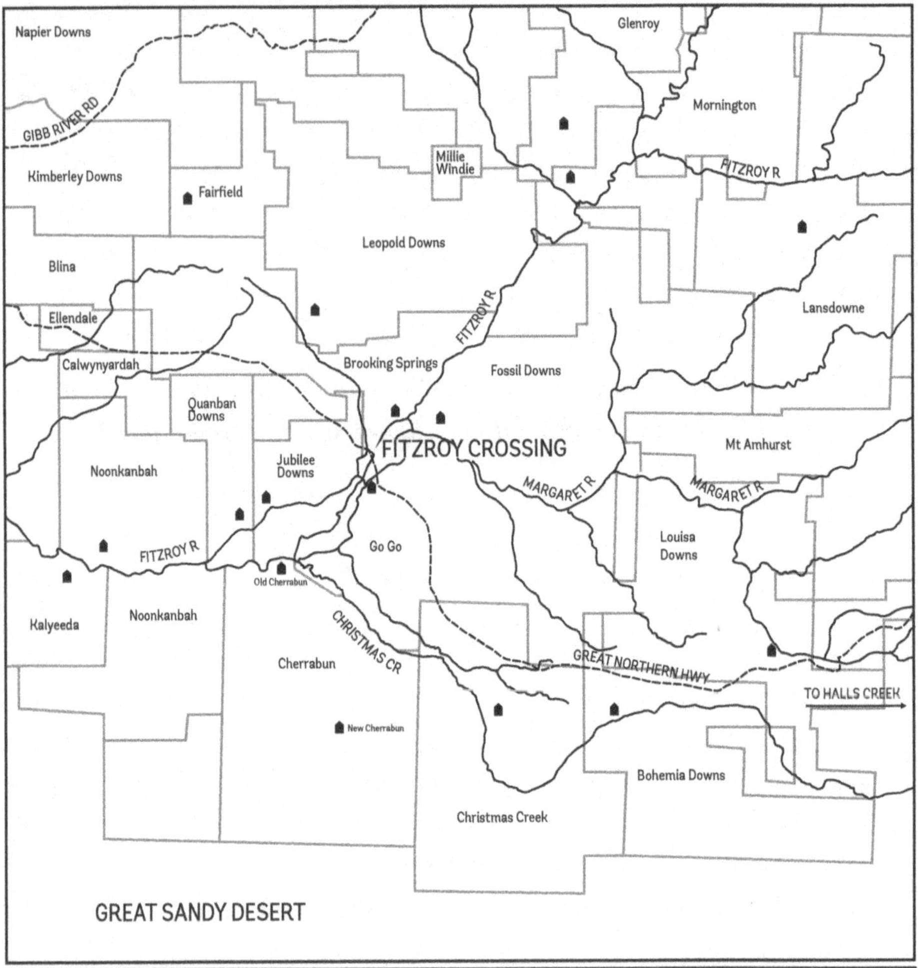

Napier Downs
Glenroy
GIBB RIVER RD
Mornington
Millie Windie
FITZROY R
Kimberley Downs
Fairfield
Leopold Downs
Blina
FITZROY R
Lansdowne
Ellendale
Calwynyardah
Brooking Springs
Fossil Downs
Quanban Downs
FITZROY CROSSING
Mt Amhurst
Noonkanbah
Jubilee Downs
MARGARET R
MARGARET R
Go Go
Louisa Downs
FITZROY R
Old Cherrabun
Kalyeeda
Noonkanbah
CHRISTMAS CR
GREAT NORTHERN HWY
Cherrabun
TO HALLS CREEK
New Cherrabun
Bohemia Downs
Christmas Creek
GREAT SANDY DESERT

REFERENCE TO AUSTRALIA
SCALE
0 10 20 30 40 50 60 70 80 90 100
Kilometres
n
KEY
PROPERTY BOUNDARY
RIVER/CREEK
MAIN ROAD
HOMESTEAD

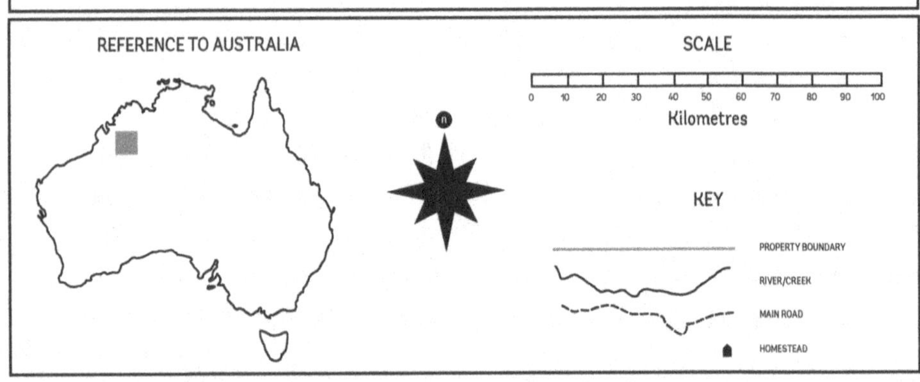

ABORIGINAL COMMUNITIES OF THE FITZROY VALLEY

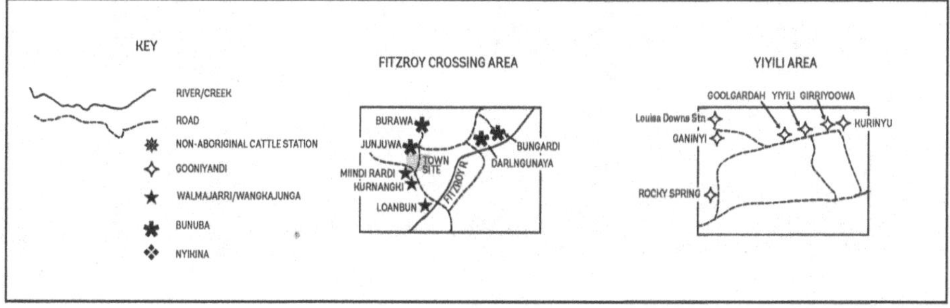

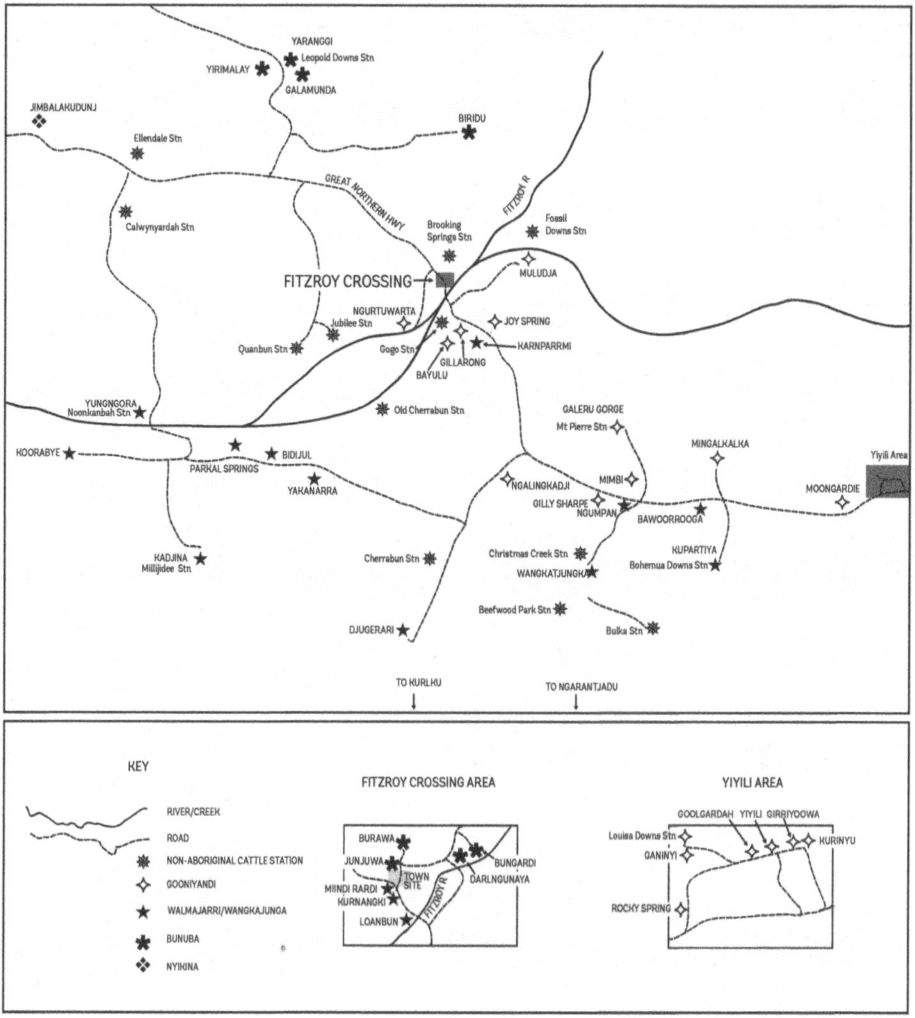

FOREWORD

Fitzroy Crossing, a town immortalised in Danny Marr's hit song 'Home Sweet Home' as that 'little one horse town that lies on the banks of the mighty Fitzroy River,' continues to defy Western logic in its ability to remain a 3,500 strong and resolute network of families that survive and flourish in remote and regional Australia.

There is an intrinsic thread that runs through the social and cultural fabric of Fitzroy Crossing and the broader Fitzroy Valley community that at first glance appears to be superficial strands of life without hope, but upon further exploration reveals a structure of humanity so vibrant, innovative and cohesive it is more akin to the innate genomes of our own being.

I was born 23 July 1960 and have grown up in the warm ambience of strong men and women who laid the foundational cultural protocols the Fitzroy Crossing community enjoys today. One side of my heritage is a dignified and revered Bunuba matriarch, the other an English orphan shipped at eleven years of age to Australia whose character was chiselled from the cobblestoned streets of Liverpool.

My earliest memories of growing up in Fitzroy Crossing, till my mid-teens, are ingrained with the images of towering proud stockmen astride their noble steeds and the women so compassionate and tender, forever exuding the protective nature of mother and teacher. My mother and father were a microcosm of the everyday struggles of the Bunuba people and their European settlers, black and white values merged yet disturbed and dictated to by a wider world of indifference and perceptions fuelled by skin colour, religion and politics.

Without doubt to define your future is to know your past. For the youth of Fitzroy Crossing to chart their own destiny, free of confusion and disillusionment, they will require an unedited portal of truth and appreciation of the cataclysmic cultural and political upheavals that occurred between the 1950s and 70s.

The author Steve Hawke, renowned and sincerely respected by the Fitzroy Valley Aboriginal Elders, masterfully blends and synchronises the external political and colonial events of the day with the extraordinarily honest and matter-of-fact recollections of Bunuba, Walmajarri, Wangkajunga, Nyikina and Gooniyandi Elders who led and coaxed their people during the roller-coaster of social and cultural transformation throughout those tumultuous decades that ensured 'A Town was Born.'

By not interfering with the verbatim of the interviewees, the author boldly invites the reader to study and interpret the stories themselves. More importantly for the sustainability of the modern-day social and cultural fabric of Fitzroy Crossing, it provides an uncensored historical account told by respected Elders interrelated to all and sundry in the Fitzroy Valley.

I hope the graphic description of events and historical footage cleverly crafted in this plethora of human tales becomes an essential orientation point for future generations in understanding how the town of Fitzroy Crossing came to be. That one hundred years from now, a leader from Bunuba, Walmajarri, Wangkajunga, Nyikina or Gooniyandi will reflect on their love of the Fitzroy Valley, that they too may be inspired to once again echo the words conveyed by my sister Olive Knight in the opening interview, which so aptly articulates the heart and soul of our communities who live on the banks of the mighty Fitzroy River.

> *It's a family town. The same thread that ran through the veins of the people in the 1960s, the same thing that has kept these people, the Fitzroy Valley people you know. The '60s didn't change anything about families, about culture, about togetherness, and having a uniqueness in voice and in the way we conduct ourselves as family and look after one another. Most of our family are gone but still that strong bond remains from the past. It didn't change. It's still there. Grog didn't take it away you know. It's still there. Running right through us.*
>
> *There's this common thread runs through. Jimbalakudunj is not a faraway country, nor is Brooking Springs or Leopold. We're all like, in this unique little town, unique little family sort of thing, and it's going to grow. It's going to stay there until we all finish you know.*

This inspiring yet grave account of how Fitzroy Crossing came to be is a testament to the courage of all those elders deceased and alive today who ventured to cross the river, had the audacity to defy the status quo and dared to dream of a better life and future for themselves and their children.

Joe Ross, Bunuba Leader

THE STORYTELLERS

George Brooking

George is a senior Bunuba elder, lawman and singer. He was born on Brooking Springs Station in 1930. In his working days he was a renowned horseman and stockman. He worked on many stations, but mainly Leopold Downs and Brooking Springs, where he was head stockman for many years. George has held many leadership positions, including as chairman of the Kimberley Aboriginal Law and Cultural Centre. In 2008 he performed as the singer in the *Jandamarra* stage play at the Perth International Arts Festival. He was the founder of Bungardi Community, a Bunuba outstation on Brooking Springs, 5 kilometres from Fitzroy Crossing, where he still lives.

Joe Brown

Joe is a Walmajarri man born at Noonkanbah in 1948. In his early years his family lived in the bush near Christmas Creek Station. He grew up on Go Go Station, and as a young man worked as a stockman there, and at Cherrabun, Ellendale, Jubilee Downs, and at Meda Station near Derby. He has been the chairman of Junjuwa, Ngurtawarta and Kurnangki communities. Joe has become a widely respected leader and cultural figure, serving as the chairman of the Kimberley Aboriginal Law and Cultural Centre for nine years. Joe lives in the Kurnangki Community in Fitzroy Crossing.

Topsy Chestnut

Topsy is a Gooniyandi woman, born in 1949 on her father's country at Louisa Downs. Her first memories are from Chestnut Bore, which was a small outstation for the Emanuel group of stations, on the old highway between Go Go and Christmas Creek. She then lived at Go Go where she was a student at the 'cave school' in the 1950s, before working as a domestic at Go Go homestead. She moved with her family to Fossil Downs, and then in the early 1970s to the United Aborigines Mission in Fitzroy Crossing. In the late 1970s and early 1980s she worked in the Fitzroy Crossing office of the Department for Community Welfare at a time when it was engaged in pioneering community development work. In the 1990s she was one of the founders of the Ngalingkadji Community, located near Chestnut Bore, where she still lives.

Jean Cox

Jean is a Gooniyandi woman who was born in 1945 on Go Go Station where she grew up. With her husband Sam Cox she has lived and worked on Go Go, Cherrabun and Louisa Downs stations. In the 1990s they moved from Bayulu to Yiyili Community, and then established an outstation at Moongardie, on Louisa Downs.

Sandy Cox

Sandy is a Walmajarri man. He was born at Mulan (Lake Gregory Station) in the south east Kimberley in 1943. As a young boy he was taken to the government settlement at Moola Bulla Station near Halls Creek. When Moola Bulla was closed down in 1955 he went to Christmas Creek Station where his parents lived, and worked as a stockman. He became a leading hand and bore worker on the Emanuel Brothers' stations Christmas Creek and Go Go. In the early 1960s, he was one of the handful of Indigenous men in the region to apply for and receive citizenship. In the 1970s he worked at Leopold Downs for a time, before moving to Bayulu. Sandy established Karnparrmi, a small outstation near Bayulu, where he lives today.

June Davis

June was born in 1956 on Fossil Downs Station where she grew up in her Gooniyandi country. She became a reluctant boarder at the United Aborigines Mission girls' hostel in Fitzroy Crossing for her schooling, then lived again at Fossil Downs, before she and her family moved into the Mission in 1975. With her husband Mervyn Street she has lived at Yiyili, Girriyoowa, and now at Muludja, on the bank of the Margaret River, where she assists at the school, and plays an active role in community and Gooniyandi affairs.

Stella Jimbidie

Stella is a Walmajarri woman born in 1943 at Old Cherrabun Station on the Fitzroy River, near where Yakanarra Community is today. In the 1950s the Cherrabun homestead was relocated away from the river to Djugareri, where Stella had her first two children, and lived until the 1969 walk off. In the late 1960s and early 1970s she worked at Quanbun, Jubilee, Nerrima, Millijidee and Noonkanbah stations, and in the years since has lived at Junjuwa, Yakanarra and Loanbung. She worked at the old hospital before it was relocated to the town site, and as a cleaner at the Department for Community Welfare. She now lives in the Fitzroy Crossing town site with her daughter and grandchildren, but also spends time at Yakanarra.

Olive Knight

Olive is a Walmajarri woman who also has Bunuba heritage. She was born at Bohemia Downs Station in 1946, and in her youth lived there, at Chestnut Bore, and then at Go Go Station. Her primary education was at the United Aborigines Mission School in Fitzroy Crossing and at Go Go School. As an adult she has completed a Diploma in Pastoral Ministries, a Certificate in Health Worker Practices, and a BA in Applied Science. She is a fluent reader and writer of Walmajarri, and an accredited interpreter/translator; she helped to write the first version of the Walmajarri dictionary. As a missionary with her first husband Jimmy Bieunderry, she lived and worked in Carnarvon and in Papua New Guinea. In recent years she has started a new career as a blues singer and performer. In 2011 she appeared in Hugh Jackman's *Back on Broadway* show in New York. Olive lives at Wangkatjunka Community, where she works in the school.

Annette Kogolo

Annette is a Walmajarri Juwaliny woman born at Go Go Station in 1959. When her father got a job at the Go Go School in the 1960s, the station manager insisted that they must leave the Go Go Station camp, and the family moved to a place of their own adjacent to the school. Like Topsy Chestnut, in the late 1970s and early 1980s she worked in the Fitzroy Crossing office of the Department for Community Welfare at a time when it was engaged in pioneering community development work. She has gone on to have a diverse career, working for a wide range of Aboriginal organisations, as a radio broadcaster, and a freelance consultant. She is on the boards of Mangkaja Arts and the Association of Northern, Kimberley and Arnhem Aboriginal Artists. She lives at Karnparrmi Community on the Great Northern Highway.

Tommy May

Tommy is a Walmajarri man. He was born at Yarrnkurnja in the Great Sandy Desert in 1935. He came in from the desert to Christmas Creek Station. When he was a boy his family lived at Meda Station near Derby. He worked as a stockman on many Kimberley stations, and spent some time working as a drover in the Kimberley and Northern Territory. As an adult, he learned to read and write both English and Walmajarri. He is a cultural leader, singer and dancer. He is also a painter and printmaker, and has been a deputy chairman of Mangkaja Arts, and chairman of the Kimberley Aboriginal Law and Cultural Centre and the Association of Northern, Kimberley and Arnhem Aboriginal Artists. He lives at the Mindi Rardi Community in Fitzroy Crossing.

Joy Nuggett

Joy is a Walmajarri woman born at Go Go Station in 1962, three years after her sister Annette. Like Annette, after the family was evicted from the station camp, she lived in a family camp established adjacent to the school. Joy completed high school in Perth, then worked at the Fitzroy Crossing kindergarten and for many years at the hospital. With her husband Jimmy Shandley, she has lived at Mount Pierre, Eight Mile (Joy Springs) and Bayulu. They now live in a station house near the old 'cave school' on Go Go Station. Joy's short story 'Break a Leg!' was published in the anthology *Kimberley Stories* (Fremantle Press, 2012).

Kevin Oscar

Kevin Oscar is a Bunuba man, born at Brooking Springs Station in 1957. He is a light aircraft and helicopter pilot who has worked as a stockman and contractor around the Kimberley. When the Bunuba people acquired Leopold Downs Station in 1991 he was the station manager for a number of years. He is currently living in his wife's home town of Halls Creek, working at a local mine.

Jimmy Shandley

Jimmy is a Gooniyandi man, born on Go Go Station in 1953. He went to school at Go Go, but was unable to fulfil his dream of further education as an apprentice mechanic. Instead, he went on to become the youngest head stockman on Go Go, and led a working life in the pastoral industry on Indigenous and non-Indigenous stations, and as an independent contractor. In the 1990s he was the manager of Mount Pierre Station. He lives with his wife Joy Nuggett in a station house near the old 'cave school' on Go Go Station.

Mervyn Street

Mervyn is a Gooniyandi man born on Louisa Downs Station in 1948. He had no schooling, and started work young as a stockman and drover. As a young man he travelled extensively, working in the Pilbara, Murchison and Goldfields regions before returning home. Mervyn is an author, illustrator, carver and painter, and a past chairman of Mangkaja Arts in Fitzroy Crossing. Mervyn was one of the founders of the Yiyili Community on Louisa Downs, and later established a smaller outstation from Yiyili at Girriyoowa. He continues his work as an artist, and is now living at the Muludja Community with his wife June Davis.

Harry Yungabun

Harry is a Walmajarri man born at New Cherrabun Station (Djugareri) in 1961. He was still a boy in 1969 when his people left the station. He grew up at the United Aborigines Mission, and at the Fig Tree Camp that evolved into Kurnangki Community. He left school at fifteen to work. While still a teenager he moved to Noonkanbah, and became the first community bookkeeper there, working with the Marra Worra Worra Resource Centre, a position he held for many years. In the 1990s he was elected to the inaugural ATSIC Regional Council. Since 2004 he has worked in the field of community and environmental health with the Nindilingarri Cultural Health Service, living for a time in Fitzroy Crossing, before moving back to Djugareri. He has also served as the chairman of Marra Worra Worra.

PREFACE

This project was conceived by Joe Ross, a leader of the Bunuba Community in Fitzroy Crossing. He believed it was important to tell the story of how today's town took shape. The seminal period was the 1960s and 70s, a period of upheaval in the pastoral industry that saw the Nyikina, Gooniyandi, Walmajarri and Wangkajunga peoples who lived and worked on the sheep and cattle stations of the Fitzroy Valley flood into the tiny township. An accommodation was reached between the Bunuba, who are the traditional owners of the town, and the newcomers. This accommodation grew into a spirit of cooperation and solidarity between the peoples of the Valley that has endured for fifty years, and has been fundamental to the way the town has grown and taken shape. I was familiar with this story through my long association with the communities of the Valley, that began in 1978, and continues still, and was delighted to be asked to undertake the work.

There were two primary sources for telling the story: the people themselves, and the official record. The first-hand accounts from the group of people I have called the Storytellers provide the heart and the core of this book. This material was collected during two stints, in November 2008 and April 2009. Some of this was done in a two-day group session at the

Karrayili Adult Education Centre, but mostly I sat down with individuals or couples in their camps, switched on a recorder, and yarned. I thank all of these people warmly, and apologise to the many others who had stories to tell, but whom I did not get to, for reasons of time and budget constraints.

Researching the official record was primarily a matter of many, many hours in the State Records Office in Perth, reading through close to one hundred files of the old Department of Native Welfare. Other files that were originally housed in the Fitzroy Crossing and Derby offices of Department of Native Welfare (DNW) were accessed through the Department's current incarnation, the Department for Child Protection (DCP), though these were heavily redacted to remove all individual names.

Essentially this book is my best effort to synthesise these two strands into a coherent account of the story I was asked to tell; the story of how a remarkable little town in the central Kimberley, that I dearly love, came to be like it is.

It is a tribute to a remarkable generation of leaders who grew up in the semi-feudal world of the Kimberley pastoral industry of the early to mid 1900s, and had the courage and vision to create a new world when that old one collapsed. We hear from a handful of them in this book—Ginger Nganawilla, Mick Nicki, Chum Lee and Michael Angelo. There were many others. To me, it was a privilege to know them and work for them in my early years in Fitzroy Crossing.

Steve Hawke

CONTENTS

INTRODUCTION

It's a family town. The same thread that ran through the veins of the people in the 1960s, the same thing that has kept these people, the Fitzroy Valley people you know. The '60s didn't change anything about families, about culture, about togetherness, and having a uniqueness in voice and in the way we conduct ourselves as family and look after one another. Most of our family are gone but still that strong bond remains from the past. It didn't change. It's still there. Grog didn't take it away you know. It's still there. Running right through us.

There's this common thread runs through. Jimbalakudunj is not a faraway country, nor is Brooking Springs or Leopold. We're all like, in this unique little town, unique little family sort of thing, and it's going to grow. It's going to stay there until we all finish you know.

Olive Knight, Wangkatjungka Community

The 1960s are remembered as a time of change and upheaval throughout the Western world, including Australia. No part of the country changed more in that decade than the remote pastoral regions of the north. But in these tropical parts the winds of change did not bring the anti-war movement, the counterculture, feminism, or the other issues that preoccupied the cities. Rather, they blew down an industry, a regime, a culture that for the best part of a century had thrived on a semi-feudal system of co-dependence between the all-powerful station bosses, and large communities of unpaid Aboriginal workers and their families.

And nowhere were the changes more profound than in the Fitzroy Valley, where many hundreds of Aboriginal people lived on a swathe of cattle stations from Noonkanbah in the west to Louisa Downs in the east, from Christmas Creek and Cherrabun on the fringe of the Great Sandy Desert to the south, to Leopold Downs and Fossil Downs butting up against the King Leopold Ranges to the north.

This is a story about those times and the dramatic changes that saw a new town come into existence.

CHAPTER ONE FITZROY CROSSING 1965

I was a drover, you know. The last droving we had from Louisa to this place, in Mindi Rardi hill there behind. You see big dust coming in that road, well that's the cattle truck and for me first time I see cattle truck, you know. And I couldn't believe, all this cattle going to go on the truck. And we take all the cattle in the yard, that yard there. You can see the post still there, the trucking yard behind there, and that's where I seen with my eyes, and that's the first time I see the cattle truck.

Mervyn Street, Muludja Community

The year is 1965. From the stations to the east like Louisa Downs, the drovers still bring the cattle in, poking slowly along the old stock routes as they have for seventy years. But now, when they cross the Fitzroy River at Donkey Crossing, instead of following the river all the way to Derby, they turn the mob north to the new yards and race on Plum Plain, opposite where Mindi Rardi Community now stands. The cattle are loaded onto trucks, and the last leg of their journey to the meatworks takes hours

Mervyn Street at the remains of the Fitzroy Crossing trucking yard with his painting depicting a bygone era.

instead of weeks. It won't be long until the droving days are over.

The nearest town of Derby is 160 miles to the west, but it seems a lot closer than it used to be. The old dirt road has recently been upgraded to bitumen under the Beef Roads scheme.

An all-weather bridge over the Fitzroy River is still many years away. Just past the new yards, the highway takes a left-hand bend, and sweeps in a two-mile arc through the empty bush, down to the old low level crossing. There is little to see: no Mindi Rardi or Kurnangki communities; no roadhouses, town site or shopping centre; no Junjuwa village. You might catch a glimpse of the United Aborigines Mission (UAM) about a half a mile off the road. Unless you take the turnoff to the Crossing Inn, the first buildings you will see are the small cluster perched between the road and the high northern bank of the river, right there at the crossing.

There is the police station and residence, the post office with residence out the back, and the relatively new addition to the town, the Australian Inland Mission hospital, which is really a nursing post, with a visiting doctor from Derby. And apart from a few sheds and ramshackle bough shades and humpies,* that is it.

There is a mail plane once a week, and a manual telephone exchange with two lines at the post office. Crackly short-wave radio is the only way to keep up with the news. The crossing can go underwater for months at a time in a big Wet, and when that happens Fitzroy becomes the end of the road. If the white stockmen from Go Go Station on the other side of the river are thirsty enough, they might make their way to the far bank and hail the hotel. One of the men working at the pub will row across, chest gleaming with sweat, angling against the current, and bring them back to slake their thirsts at the bar.

---

* *'Killer' is the term used for a station beast slaughtered and butchered for local consumption.*

When you can get over the crossing, the next stop is Halls Creek, 190 miles to the east, and dirt road all the way. The bitumen ends at Fitzroy Crossing. It is a tiny, remote, isolated settlement. It would be a gross exaggeration to call it a town. It really hasn't changed much since it stuttered into being in the 1890s.

The nearest office of the State Government's Department of Native Welfare (DNW) is in Derby. In this remote corner of Western Australia, 1,500 miles from Perth, the Department's influence over the lives of the 'natives', for good or ill, is limited. But following a pattern that has been in operation for thirty years they conduct regular patrols of the district and compile detailed reports.

In April of 1965 they list twenty-three 'natives' as living in Fitzroy Crossing Town. Ten are employed at the hotel, one at the police station; there are four pensioners; six children and two 'others'.

> *The employed people at the Hotel are provided fully with clothing, blankets and food. Pensioners care for themselves. Children attend school at the United Aborigines Mission. The camp consists of 6* [corrugated iron] *huts with earth floors. These buildings are reasonably sound but primitive. Two E.C.* [pit] *toilets are provided.*[1]

As is the style of these reports, an appendix lists all twenty-three people: surname, Christian name, sex, caste (F.B. for full blood, H.C. for half caste and so forth), birth date, relationship, occupation and weekly wage.

The wages for the men working at the Crossing Inn range from one to three pounds a week, for the women from one pound to two pounds ten shillings. A woman working at the police station earns one pound a week. The basic wage for males at the time under State Awards is fifteen pounds and nineteen shillings a week.[2]

The report comments on the condition of the camp near the hotel:

> *The camp area was littered with tins and bottles ... Numerous dogs were present and several pigs were in the camp ... The inhabitants were spoken to and advised that if they wished to remain at Fitzroy, a higher standard was required and necessary ... The Hotel disclaims any responsibility for the camp.*[3]

And a handwritten footnote touches on a controversy of the time as to whether or not this camp should be tolerated. Some were advocating a reserve should be established in the vicinity and living conditions improved. Others were arguing for the camp to be closed down and the residents relocated. The DNW officer opts for the status quo, whereby no-one needs to take responsibility: 'The provision and equipping of a reserve in the area is impractical ... Closure of the area would cause economic hardship and loss of a social amenity.'[4]

For almost sixty years the 'three Ps'—pub, police station and post office—made up the little settlement at the Fitzroy River Crossing. In 1950 a new establishment arrived, the Fitzroy Crossing Native Depot. It was removed from the established settlement by a good couple of miles.

The Depot seemed to be a victim of mixed motivations. A new and zealous DNW officer fresh from New Guinea envisaged it as a training institution for the pastoral industry. His seniors seemed to see it as a replacement for the faltering ration station at Udialla, 125 miles to the west, while a clipping in one of the DNW files says, 'The institution will cater for natives who wander in from desert country in search of food and tobacco. While feeding and accommodating the wandering natives, the station will soften their first real impact with white people and prepare them for absorption into the pastoral industry.'[5]

From the outset the Depot struggled with staff and resources. By 1952 the Commissioner was writing an urgent recommendation to his Minister that the Department should hand over the Depot to the UAM, headquartered in Melbourne, 'to continue the work as a Children's Home and general mission', and in the same year control was handed to the UAM, and the Depot became the Mission.[6]

Occasional inspections of the Mission were made by DNW, but it did not need to take the initiative in keeping track of numbers. The Mission survived on the subsidies it received from the Department, and generated astounding amounts of paperwork to justify this income, with the Commissioner in Perth keeping a keen eye on it at all times.

Perhaps the most remarkable entry in dozens of files that take up feet of shelf space in the state archives of Western Australia is a memo from the Commissioner to the Mission superintendent regarding the rations issued to the 'inmates'. It is a detailed list of the weekly rations to be issued to each 'indigent'. The list includes 'Haricot Beans, Baked Beans (tin), Peas (tin) and Split Peas' but contains the rider: 'Where you have five different kinds of peas, please issue one kind only to each person—this may be varied on succeeding ration days. That is to say, one native is not to receive five different kinds of beans each week.'[7]

The files remain silent, but one can only hope the Mission superintendent took such important instructions from Perth to heart.

Through the years, the Mission remained assiduous with its paperwork, as required to generate the funds required for its survival. Twice a year a 'Register of Inmates' was submitted.

The register for June of 1965 lists 135 inmates.[8] There are families, pensioners, indigents, and a handful listed as employed. But the large majority of the inmates are the children of men and women working on the stations of the Fitzroy Valley. The Mission receives a subsidy of

BJB/TM
20th August, 1952.

The Superintendent,
United Aborigines Mission,
FITZROY CROSSING.

Dear Sir,

re Handover Statements.

Attached hereto please find forms in respect to items in your store as at the date of handover. Would you please check these forms and sign the original of each and return to this office.

As concerns your indigent rations stocks, it has been decided to transfer those items as per Form 37 Sheet 2 from your store to the Indigent Ration Store. As no doubt Mr. Redfern has explained the necessity of accounting for these stores, would you please issue them on the following scale.

Haricot Beans Baked Beans (tin) Peas (tin) Split Peas	}	Same scale as B.B. Peas
Cornflour Custard powder	}	Same scale as B. Powder
S.R. Flour	-	1 lb. with 7 lb. of plain.
Fish	-	Please issue with meat - not to exceed 3 lb per week total weight
Jellies	-	2 ozs per week.
Condensed Milk	-	Same issue as powdered milk.
Tapioca Pearl Barley	}	Same scale as Sago.
Soap	-	1 tablet per week.

Where you have five different kinds of peas, please issue one kind only to each person - this may be varied on succeeding ration days. That is to say, one native is not to receive five different kinds of beans each week. This is to apply also in milk, (powdered and condensed) one type only to be issued to each individual. Similarly in sago, rice, tapioca and pearl barley, please issue, a total of ½ lb per week, not ½ lb of each food per person per week.

It is presumed that you have on hand sufficient forms 36 and 37. Kindly advise if to the contrary.

Yours faithfully,

Encls.

(S.G. Middleton)
COMMISSIONER OF NATIVE AFFAIRS.

Government letter to the United Aboriginies Mission about the distribution of rations

thirty-nine pounds per quarter for each of these children, as well as a Living Away From Home Allowance from the Education Department of seven shillings and sixpence a week. A child's mother working as a washerwoman at the Crossing Inn is earning a pound a week, or thirteen pounds a quarter. Her wage is exactly a third of what a parsimonious government is prepared to pay as a boarding fee to a bush mission.

The children are housed in dormitories, and attend a government school on the Mission grounds. The girls' dormitory is 'badly damaged by white ants'.[9] The workers and pensioners live in one-room galvanised-iron huts. The wages for those who are employed range from one pound fifteen shillings to three pounds per fortnight.

A 1966 inspection by a DNW officer contains the observations:

> *I feel that this Mission's aim is initially, to cater for Divine Welfare in an ecclesiastical world of its own and unconsciously resents any outside interference. Leaning only to those aspects of native welfare that are welcomed and fit into its religious teachings. A new admission is classed as another one for the good cause firstly and secondly as a native welfare case. In effect too much emphasis is placed on the Divine aspect and not enough on worldly welfare.*[10]

The whitefellas are not counted, listed and analysed in the same way as the 'natives'. At a guess there are four or five at the Mission and school, and at best a dozen more down near the crossing. The carefully counted natives total 158, but most of them are out of sight and out of mind up at the Mission, living on one kind of peas each week.

But this is all about to change. Across the border in the Northern Territory the Commonwealth Conciliation and Arbitration Commission is hearing an application from the Northern Australian Workers Union, arguing that Aboriginal station workers in the northern pastoral industry should receive the same wages as their white co-workers. The Commission's decision will be the catalyst for upheavals that irrevocably change the face of the Fitzroy Valley, and the tiny township of Fitzroy Crossing.

CHAPTER TWO THE BEGINNINGS

Bunuba country is a land of ranges, rivers and grassy plains that stretches from Mil̲uwindi* (the King Leopold Ranges) in the north, and Ban̲diln̲gan (Windjana Gorge) in the west, down to the mighty Fitzroy River that forms its eastern and southern boundaries.

The Fitzroy drains a basin larger in area than the state of Victoria. In the monsoon rains that pound down in the tropical wet season each summer, the glistening ranges sparkle with waterfalls, and the river swells to a mighty torrent that spills out onto the surrounding floodplains.

In the days before cattle and white men, the Bunuba's neighbours were the Gooniyandi to the east; the Ngarinyin and Andajin to the north; the Un̲ggumi and the Nyikina to the west and south west; and in the desert country to the south and south east, the Walmajarri and the Wangkajunga. The township of Fitzroy Crossing sits in the south-east corner of Bunuba country.

The first whitefella to come into this country was the explorer Alexander Forrest, the younger brother of Western Australian Premier John Forrest,

---

* *'Killer' is the term used for a station beast slaughtered and butchered for local consumption.*

in 1879. He reported that the grasslands of the Kimberley were ideal for grazing, and over the next ten years the pastoralists pressed into this new frontier.

From the south, men with dreams of riches shipped up flocks of sheep, and stations spread from the tiny new port of Derby, at the mouth of the Fitzroy River, and up the Fitzroy and Lennard Rivers. Overland through Queensland and the Northern Territory came the Duracks and their cattle to open up the first stations in the East Kimberley; they were soon followed by the McDonald brothers who established Fossil Downs Station in 1885.

In 1886 gold was found at Halls Creek, and the first rush of prospectors trekked overland to the new field from Derby, following the Fitzroy and Mary Rivers.

In 1888 Joseph Blythe established Brooking Springs Station and built the first rough homestead where the Crossing Inn now stands. Though it was just another new settler's shack, hardly fitting of the title of homestead, in hindsight, this first building in what is now known as Fitzroy Crossing can be seen as a significant moment in Australian history. Over the previous hundred years since the establishment of the first penal settlement in Sydney, the newcomers had spread around the continent, following coastlines and rivers. One branch had reached through New South Wales, north into Queensland, then westward across the Northern Territory, with Fossil Downs being the furthest outpost. The other had snaked out across the southern fringe of the continent, and up the Western Australian coast, as far as Quanbun Station.

There were still vast reaches of desert country, and wild areas like the north Kimberley where the Indigenous owners remained undisturbed. The continent was still a collection of colonies, not a country. But a century after Sydney town was founded, Blythe's homestead, with Fossil Downs as his eastern neighbour, and Quanbun to the west, represented the point at which these two branches finally met and joined, and the circle of white settlement around the Australian mainland was completed.

The 1890s was the decade in which Fitzroy Crossing was born. It was not planned or gazetted by government like the port of Derby. Like many a bush outpost, it stumbled into existence, with no clear definition of when it took on the status of a township.

Before he took up Brooking Springs, Joe Blythe had been a publican in Derby, and it seems he did more than just run cattle from his new base, even if the grog was an unofficial sideline. Mary Durack's memoir about the East Kimberley dynasty founded by her grandfather Patsy, *Kings in Grass Castles*, refers to Blythe at his 'homestead shanty cum hotel'[1] in 1893. And in 1897 an official wayside House Licence was issued in the name of Joe's son Charlie.

At first, no-one was sure what to call the emerging settlement. Blythe's place was known as the Brooking Inn and the Brooking Creek Hotel. Correspondence and records of the time refer variously to 'Upper Fitzroy', 'Fitzroy River', 'Brooking Creek' and 'Fitzroy Telegraph Station' before the name was eventually settled. But by 1895 on the north bank of the Fitzroy River, on either side of Brooking Creek, there was the pub, a telegraph station cum post office, and a police station.

The supplies for the tiny township and the surrounding stations came in creaking wagons hauled by teams of donkeys or bullocks from Derby, following the Fitzroy River or the new telegraph line that skirted the Napier and Oscar Ranges to the north. From Noonkanbah, 90 kilometres to the west, to Christmas Creek, a similar distance to the south east, there were fewer than a dozen stations. Each was a million acres or more. Except for

Fossil Downs, the owners were companies or absentee landlords, based in Perth or the eastern states. It was still very much frontier country, with a thinly spread settler population of less than a hundred.

The 1890s was also a decade of war in the Fitzroy Valley and the ranges to the north.

When the pastoralists tried to spread their reach beyond the open plains of the river country into the hill country of the Napier and Oscar Ranges they encountered fierce resistance from the Bunuba people, who were able to harry the stations and their flocks, and then retreat to the rugged limestone ranges where pursuit or tracking was near impossible.

A young Bunuba man known to the pastoralists as Pigeon, and to his people as Jandamarra, became a pivotal figure, and ultimately a legendary hero of the Kimberley.[2] He lived on both sides of the frontier, working on Lennard River and Lillimooloora stations as a boy, then going bush for his initiation. At fifteen he was jailed for allegedly spearing sheep.

Returning to Lillimooloora after five years as a prisoner and police stablehand in Derby, he formed a friendship with the white stockman, Bill Richardson. When the tactics of Jandamarra's Bunuba countrymen forced the closure of the sheep station, Richardson joined the police force, and Jandamarra became his tracker, rounding up his own people on the chain.

The team of Richardson and Pigeon brought the Bunuba resistance to its knees. In 1894 they were resting at Lillimooloora before heading into Derby, with most of the remaining Bunuba leaders as their prisoners. But Pigeon shot his friend Richardson, and returned to his people as Jandamarra. A week later he led an ambush on a party pushing through Windjana Gorge with the intention of establishing a new station deep in the heart of Bunuba country. They killed two white stockmen, and seized an arsenal of weapons and ammunition, as well as a wagonload of supplies.

It was the start of a three-year long resistance that halted pastoral expansion, and almost brought the Kimberley to a standstill. At one stage a quarter of the colony of Western Australia's police force was in the Kimberley, hunting for the elusive rebel. Fitzroy Crossing and the surrounding sheep and cattle stations felt like outposts under siege.

Hundreds of Aboriginal people were killed by the troopers hunting Jandamarra. And it was not just his Bunuba countrymen who perished. The Aboriginal oral history tells of patrols sweeping down either side of the Fitzroy, from Brooking Springs to Noonkanbah, killing as they went.

Jandamarra was finally gunned down near Tunnel Creek in 1897, at the age of just twenty-four. His death marked the end of any armed resistance to the pastoral regime and the police who acted as its enforcers. 'Myalls', to use the terminology of the era for those living a traditional life outside the authority of the station, were no longer tolerated. The Indigenous survivors had no choice but to live and work on the huge sheep and cattle stations that now occupied their lands.

CHAPTER THREE **THE EARLY DAYS**

The people that came behind those first kartiya[*] *don't know. These other people don't know. They think the kartiya was doing good in the early days. But they were doing very bad, shooting people. That's no good.*

When anybody made trouble at the station they would lock him up, give him a hiding there inside, and kill him after. They were having black women, those kartiya. They made it wrong. Her husband made a row. That woman came back from the job, and her husband asked, 'What's going on?'

'He's been pinching me from you,' his wife told him. And that man came up to the manager, he came up to the store, and walked inside there. At night time. They belted him, killed him, and took him away at night time.

That was in my time. I put everything in my brain.[1]

Ginger Nganawilla of Noonkanbah in 1978

* 'Kartiya' is a common term among Kimberley people to refer to whitefellas.

Ginger was born not long after the turn of the twentieth century, in the shadow of the decade of war in the Fitzroy Valley. A stockman and station hand all his working life, he became one of the leaders of the Noonkanbah community through the 1960s and 1970s. He was a keeper of stories from his parents' time, and grew up during the early years of the pastoral era. The stories and the personal experiences of Ginger and his contemporaries leave no doubt that those were harsh times:

> *I know what every manager was doing, on the stations all around. When he belted that man inside the house, he took him away at night time. He shot an old bullock or cow, slit the guts, picked up that man and shoved him inside. He turned it over, and nobody could see. That's what the kartiya were doing before ... This is the story from Cherrabun, Christmas Creek and Bohemia Downs, all around. We've got plenty of stories that say what the kartiya was doing before.*[2]

He was an eye-witness to a brutal attack on his own father:

> *My father, he was working on Quanbun Station. He went away from the station a little bit, he got sick and tired of work, and he went away. Old man Rose* [the owner of Quanbun] *put him into the police. They chased him along and found him halfway to Cherrabun, and grabbed him there.*
>
> *Right; tie him up. They tied up his legs, and tied up his two hands, to a tree. They got a big lump of stone, and hit him all round. All around the face, all around the ribs, low on the back. They made him proper crippled, he couldn't walk around.*

Ginger Nganawilla

I ran, crying. The police grabbed me by the neck and took hold of me right there, crying for my father.

After that, my mother. He got her on the ground and tied her up with her hands behind her back. He put his hand on her neck, and put his foot on her; stopped her crying. They crippled him properly, my father. He was cut all around ... I was a big boy, good middle size, when the police did that to my father.[3]

The elders of the 1960s and 1970s had an endless store of such stories, up to and including mass killings on the stations such as Cherrabun that border the Great Sandy Desert, that can be dated well into the 1920s.

The society that evolved from around 1900 was dominated by large sheep and cattle stations, with prime river frontage, mostly owned by companies based in Perth or elsewhere. On the southern fringes where the good country petered into desert, and to the north in the stony, less fertile range country, there were smaller stations run by battlers and 'poddy dodgers', who built their herds by poaching the unbranded poddy calves from their larger neighbours.

Large or small, running sheep or cattle, the basic model was the same. There was hardly a white woman living in the Fitzroy Valley at the time. Shearing teams would come up from the south to the big sheep stations for a few weeks each year. But most of the time the number of whitefellas on a station could be comfortably counted on the fingers of one hand. Every station needed Aboriginal labour; they could not operate without it in this remote country.

The station owners and managers essentially regarded the Aboriginal people as property, part of the station's goods and chattels. Western Australia's Aborigines Act of 1905 created a permit system under which they were licensed to employ Natives, and it was an offence for Natives to 'abscond' from employment. With the widescale conflict of the Jandamarra era behind them, enforcing these laws became a primary role for the police. And Ginger's story shows just how brutally this was done at times.

Historian Peter Biskup in his book *Not Slaves, Not Citizens* describes 'a sort of code of honour among the pastoralists not to interfere with each other's Aborigines, a runaway stockman had usually no choice but to return to his station'.[4] An example of this code in action, and of the dependence of the stations on their unpaid workers, can be found in the DNW's Leopold Downs Station file, where the officer in charge of the Fitzroy Police Station provides a detailed report of a walk off from the station in June of 1936.[5] There had been a confrontation in the station yards between the new manager of a few weeks' standing and the Aboriginal workers. The manager went to the homestead and returned with a rifle. He claimed that it was to shoot a misbehaving bullock that had been the cause of the argument.

> *A native remonstrated with him saying 'you don't want to shoot em boy. Suppose you don't want em you sack em ... In the morning when* [the manager] *awoke and called the camp he found that all the natives had left during the night, as he could not work the cattle without the natives he decided to abandon the muster.*[6]

The manager immediately made for Fitzroy to inform the police, hoping to 'induce them to return', and failing that, to notify the owners that a shipment of bullocks due to leave the station in a couple of weeks would have to be cancelled. In most parts of Western Australia in this era, the police also held office as the local 'Protector of Aborigines', and when required would report to the 'Chief Protector', who was the head of the

DNW. On this occasion the police report to the Chief Protector concludes with the comments:

> *Whatever faults of* [the manager] *which may have contributed towards making the natives run away will I am sure be rectified in the future as he quite realises that if he cannot get the natives to work for him, his own services will soon be dispensed with by the station owners as they can run the station without him, but not without the natives.*[7]

Police trackers were dispatched to find the 'runaways'. Some were persuaded to return, but others refused, and three months later, a number of families were still in the 'ration camp' attached to the police station, and the officer was having difficulty finding alternative employment for them.

> [Names deleted][*] *have expressed a desire to work on Margaret Downs (Go Go) the fact that* [name deleted] *originally came from Christmas Creek and would like to be at Margaret Downs where he would be in closer contact with his own tribe, coupled with his dislike of the present manager of Leopold Station is the reason given for desiring a change.*

> *I approached* [name deleted] *the manager of Margaret Downs ... and he informed me that he would be prepared to give the natives work provided it did not cause ill feeling between* [him and the Leopold manager].[8]

---

* *'Killer' is the term used for a station beast slaughtered and butchered for local consumption.*

A meeting between the two managers could not be arranged for some time, and the officer had no choice but to let the people stay in the ration camp.

> *I respectfully ask your approval of my action in this matter as there is no possibility of them obtaining employment at the present time as other Station managers take the same view of the matter as* [the Margaret Downs manager] ...
>
> *I do not wish to give you the impression that all Station Managers in this district would boycott a native from obtaining employment merely because he had run away from another Station, but few if any of them would be inclined to put such a native on without first discussing the matter with the previous employer for fear that it would be said that they induced the native.*[9]

The constable concludes this report by saying:

> *I think most present day Station Managers realise that the native is a free agent to come and go as he pleases and with few exceptions are satisfied that that is only fair and reasonable.*[10]

But despite this, and despite the relaxation of the harsher aspects of the 1905 legislation about absconding, the 'code' so clearly identified in the policeman's reports effectively meant that Aboriginal people had very limited freedom of movement. There were no missions or other settlements in the Fitzroy Valley at this time. The ration camp at the police station was only for 'indigents'. The officer in charge had to justify all and any people staying there, and acquit all sorts of paperwork to the Department in Perth in order to receive the rations subsidy. And he was always eager to move people out of the camp back to the stations.

A memo from the Fitzroy police in December 1945 to the Commissioner of Native Affairs reports that:

> *Recently Constable Napier made a patrol of the Fitzroy River south from this Station, during which a number of natives were accosted and brought back to the Station. Some of these natives had run away from their employment on Stations and some were indigent and in poor condition. The absconding natives have been returned to their employers and the indigents placed on temporary rations, pending your approval.*[11]

The language and the actions of the patrol could have come from 1915.

Walmajarri elder Joe Brown gives a different perspective on the patrols and the ration camp at the police station:

> *When policemen bin go out, patrol, you know, they used to go out looking for people what's bin run away from station, they had a list of people's names from station manager and then they used to go out ...* [when] *people bin meet up law time. They would sneak in, come out, grab em that lot now, tie em up longa chain. And all that lot police boys know that lot prisoners. Take em in that station and ... might be two, three people, got to trouble, they take em all away.*

Maybe about 1,000 people bin in that old police station. Right, the manager, he used to come around looking for people to work. They go to police station look em. 'Oh, he's a strong man.' Pick em all the strong people. That's what they bin do ...

Station mob and all these river people. And they might have run away ... [Or] *they send that man, trouble maker, when that kartiya can handle him ...*

Old police station ... Those people never bin locked up inside ... They used to just tell em, 'If you run away again we got to shoot you.' Or something like that. They used to just stay there.

Joy Shandley recalls the powers of the police and station managers over people's lives:

People were being placed on other people's country. I think it was the police who had more control. And the station managers, they were like policemen themselves. They say, 'Okay, I'll take you and your family, place you over on Christmas Creek, or you can go to Cherrabun,' you know. They had no choice, they just had to go. Like we were saying, how did they go into these stations? Maybe it was too overcrowded at Christmas Creek so some of them were moved to Go Go Station, because of the manager's opinion.

The vast majority of Aboriginal people in the Valley had to make the best of their lot, and if the manager was particularly harsh, hope that he might move on. And they were expected to be obedient, and to work hard.

Noonkanbah elder Joe Wunmah has told of how 'he was "given a good hiding" by his parents, so that "when kartiya tell me to do rough work, give no cheek, do it".'[12]

CHAPTER FOUR THE DESERT MOB

We were following the creek, chasing cattle, oh, good fresh ones. We all came along, and then made a camp. Two blokes came along, found us. 'Oh Christ, big mob of people here.' They went back and told that kartiya.

The next night, a long way before daylight, they came. One station kartiya, mob of police boys, and Christmas Creek boys.

Finish.

I got out, I was a little one. My old man took me away, we ran up a hill. Oh, we heard shots. Bang, bang. They started shooting all the people. With the little kids they only used a stick. Kill them, hit them on the head. I was a young feller then ...

They used kerosene, burned them up. Big mob of people. Too much. Too much.

Mick Nicki of Noonkanbah, 1978[1]

Mick Nicki

Mick Nicki and his family were desert people, from the country to the south of Kalijidi (the St George Ranges). The massacre Mick survived happened at Timber Creek near the southern boundary of what was then Cherrabun Station. Afterwards, he and his family lived for a while longer in the St George Ranges that lie on Cherrabun and Millijidee stations, but eventually they came in and lived on Noonkanbah Station. In DNW files, Mick's year of birth is given as 1925. Even if that estimate was wrong, by comparing his age to other elders of the time, and the information he gave, the earliest possible date for the massacre would be about 1920, but it seems more likely to have been around 1930.

Once the war with Jandamarra and the Bunuba people was over and the river country in the Kimberley was pacified, from the turn of the twentieth century, most of the stories of conflict and killing come from Millijidee, Cherrabun, Christmas Creek and Bohemia Downs; the stations that bordered the Great Sandy Desert to the south of Fitzroy Crossing. This was the new frontier. But this time, it was Aboriginal people moving out of their country, into lands now controlled by the whitefellas. Between the 1920s and the 1960s the Walmajarri and Wangkajunga peoples left their desert lands.

Many of the stories of this time are told as first-hand accounts in *Out of the Desert: Stories from the Walmajarri Exodus.*[2] The introduction to this book explains some of the reasons for this migration.

> *Over time the Walmajarri people who lived closest to the cattle and sheep stations were drawn towards them out of economic interest and a desire to sample new goods ... Many new arrivals lived at first as fringe-dwellers on the stations, camping in the hills, hunting, poaching cattle, and covertly receiving station goods such as flour and tobacco from their settled relations. Later they chose or were forced to work for the station owners.*

> *News of this different life spread to their more remote relations, who gradually followed their countrymen to take up the mixed blessings of the stations. Despite the deep ambivalence some desert people must have felt about leaving their country and everything that had given their life meaning, eventually all of them left. The last scattered groups that arrived on stations in the late 1960s had no alternative, for their society had so dwindled that it could no longer be sustained.*[3]

The stations welcomed this new source of labour, but would not tolerate the 'fringe dwellers'. The desert folk had to forego their independence, and any freedom to come and go. Otherwise they faced the might of the stations and police.

Mick Nicki told gleeful stories of herding Millijidee sheep up against fences, killing them en masse, and taking only the fattest to eat. But this was followed by tales of police raids, marches in neck chains,* relations walking back to their country after stints in Broome jail, and one incident where he wore the neck chains himself as a young man.[4]

In *Out of the Desert* Boxer Yankarr tells a story similar to that of Mick Nicki; of escaping a mass shooting, being taken to Christmas Creek Station, being taken bush by his mother, returning to desert-living and spearing cattle, and repeated police raids, before he finally settled at Cherrabun, and left the desert behind.[5]

These incidents of killings on the desert fringe in the early part of the twentieth century do not appear in any of the official or historical records. They appear to have been carried out by white station personnel, without

---

* For many decades, in the remote regions of Western Australia, it was common practice for Indigenous prisoners, captured by the police on horseback patrols, to be placed on a long chain with each prisoner having a loop of chain around his neck, attached to the main chain. This way they were able to walk the long distances to their place of imprisonment.

police involvement, and clearly there was a code of silence among the perpetrators.

By the 1940s it seems the days of indiscriminate killing of the desert people had come to an end, but not the tensions and troubles. In May of 1942 the manager at Christmas Creek, Frank English, wrote a three-page letter to the Fitzroy Crossing police with a detailed account of difficulties he was encountering with a man he called Warri.

> *He is a troublemaker, has three gins and is a head among blacks ... His tribe runs out into the desert to Godfrey's Tank. He continually runs away from jobs given him on stations ... Warri through his tribal leadership makes the younger boys get up to mischief. One young bush blackfellow came into the station camp and interfered with a gin ... Last night Warri paid a night visit to the camp with the same young blackfellow ... They got hold of one our stockboy's gins and Warri himself dragged her to a creek a mile away. This will probably end in a fight with spears ...*
>
> *I hope you can put this matter right and give Warri his just desserts. He would be better shifted to another country where he can't return for fear of being speared or a good long stretch in jail.*[6]

The next entry in the file is a closely typed two-page report from the Fitzroy constable to the Commissioner of Native Affairs, headed 'Troublesome natives at Christmas Creek'. The report details the constable's patrol, his raid on Warri's camp at sundown, bringing the group into Fitzroy, and his interrogations, including that of Boxer Yankarr, who it seems had returned to the bush after seven years on Cherrabun Station. Boxer and another man were returned to Cherrabun, while Warri and others were held at the Ration Camp. The constable reports:

> *It seems that for a number of years managers of Christmas Creek Station have almost been forced to supply the desert tribe frequenting the district with a certain amount of food ... Under the influence of leaders of the Warri type, members of this tribe become very cheeky, and it appears that something will have to be done, either by supplying rations from this Station, or incurring expense to have this area visited by motor car fairly frequently to deal with the ringleaders.*[7]

The constable is adamant that future patrols should be by motor car; as he put it, 'I have been out of the saddle for a good number of years ... I was several days getting over it, and I don't feel inclined to repeat the effort at the present time'. He writes that: 'The bush natives in that district [are] almost becoming a menace to the whites on the Station', and concludes, 'As Warri and his kind evidently have sufficient cunning to force the younger members of the tribe to do the "dirty work" and also possess some tribal influence over them, and also the stockboys, it appears to me that their presence should be removed if possible.'[8]

Commissioner Neville then writes to the Minister for the North-West, naming Warri and four others, and stating: 'I deem it necessary to submit a recommendation to you that [they] should be removed to Moola Bulla Native Station and detained there under disciplinary control.'[9]

He also recommends the 'issue of warrants for the capture and removal to Moola Bulla' of three other men who had eluded the constable's patrol. As Chief Protector, Neville had legal power over the lives of Aboriginal people in many different ways, including determining where they must live. Moola Bulla, just north west of Halls Creek, was a cattle station run by DNW, and used as both a ration station, and an informal prison. Neville's letter also argues strongly against the suggestion of a ration station at Christmas Creek on the grounds of expense, and urges an increase in police patrols, preferably mounted.[10]

The recommended warrants were quickly issued, followed by a flurry of correspondence about the easiest and cheapest way of removing Warri and the others to Moola Bulla, until a haulage contractor turned up in town saying that he had instructions to take them.

> *I handed over the natives concerned to Mr Sharpe, together with the warrants, and in order to assure the safe custody of the male prisoners through their own country, Mr Sharpe placed them on the chain. I have no idea what view you take of this procedure, but I can assure you that it was quite necessary to secure these natives.*[11]

This incident in 1942 is possibly the latest on record in Western Australia of Aboriginal prisoners being 'placed on the chain'. These were men and women who had not been charged with any offence, and were being summarily removed from their country into 'disciplinary control' by Ministerial order. The Commissioner responded with an endorsement of the action: 'you had no option in respect to securing them by means of neck chains'.[12]

Soon afterwards the three men for whom arrest warrants had been issued were also removed to Moola Bulla, along with 'three gins' and 'five small children'.[13]

Subsequent entries on the file show that the whole group 'absconded from Moola Bulla in March 1943'. One man was found working on Brooking Springs, 300 kilometres away near Fitzroy Crossing, and allowed to stay there. Another was sent to the Derby Leprosarium, and the others were 'apprehended and returned to Moola Bulla in November 1943'. One of Warri's wives died suddenly at Moola Bulla in 1946. There is intermittent correspondence and notes about the status of the others, and then in July 1946 the Commissioner writes to the manager at Moola Bulla:

> *If you consider that the period of their detention has served to sufficiently punish them, and they could be returned to their district without much fear of a repetition of their menacing behaviour, I am willing to give consideration to their return. However, removals in the Kimberley are an expensive item against the Department's finances, and this aspect has to be kept in mind when giving attention to any further expense the Department may incur in allowing leniency to these natives.*[14]

The Fitzroy Crossing policeman, by now a sergeant, is opposed to their release, saying: 'The males in this group are a bad type and I am afraid their return to their former surroundings may involve your Department in a good deal of expense later on, as it is most likely that they will again become troublesome.'[15]

After that, the file falls silent. But, apart from their months on the run in 1943, for at least four years, the survivors were imprisoned without charge in a place which was like a foreign country for them, with their ongoing detention being as much about the cost of transporting them 150 kilometres home, as about their suitability for release or otherwise.

One of Warri's 'ringleaders' in this affair is named as Limerick. This man

Commissioner of Native Affairs.

Re. Escort of Native Prisoners. 308/30.McB/B.

In reply to your letter of the 26th.ult.. I have to advise that all natives in respect of whom warrants were issued have now been arrested.

Just prior to receiving the above letter, Mr.D. M.(Bert) Sharpe, haulage contractor for Moola Bulla Native Station, called at this Station and informed me that he had been instructed by Mr.A.George, Officer in Charge of Moola Bulla, to pick up the natives held under warrant for removal to Moola Bulla. I naturally concluded that these instructions had originated at your Office, as I had not communicated with Mr.George in connection with them. I handed over the natives concerned to Mr.Sharpe, together with the warrants, and in order to assure the safe custody of the male prisoners through their own country, Mr Sharpe placed them on the chain. I have no idea of what view you take of this proceedure, but I can assure you that it was quite necessary to secure these natives. My own opinion is that, where a chain is used on natives, a Police Officer or some person employed by your Department should be in attendance.

Constable Mason went to Christmas Creek Station on the 2nd.inst. and was successful in apprehending Nammie @ Coco, and Yungur @ Possum. On the morning of the 9th.inst. I raided the Station camp at Cherrabun and apprehended Agamal @ Pindan Jack. I found the latter with three gins, Dalgur, Egimia, and Coolgarra. and five small children aged from approximately six years to a few days. With Quingie @ Pindan on three months probation at Christmas Creek Station, where he is giving satisfaction at the present time, this completes the removal of the cause of trouble from the vicinity of the Station as reported by Mr.Max.English, manager, who incidently has left this district on and extended holiday. Christmas Creek Station is on the edge of the desert, and will probably always be subjected to annoyance by the bad blackfellow who makes his home on the desert.

The six adult natives and the five children, referred to above, will be transferred to Moola Bulla as early as possible.

I note your remarks regarding the observance of economy in connection with matters relating to natives. I shall do my utmost to help you in this regard. I have no motor vehicle of my own, neither has Constable Mason, as a matter of fact there is not a serviceable motor vehicle nearer than Leopold Downs, which is 25 miles away. The hiring of a motor vehicle does not benefit me financially, and it is only when I consider it the common sense thing to do that I would approach you for approval to hire one.

Fitzroy Crossing
11th. Sept. 1942.

Constable 1524.

Letter to Commissioner Neville detailing escort of Moola Bulla prisoners

was Limerick Malyapuka Pindan, who would become a senior leader at Looma Community between Fitzroy Crossing and Derby, where many of the desert mob settled. He was a renowned songman, and one of the leaders of the push by the desert people to return to country that gained momentum in the 1990s. As a blind old man in 1993, he was able to give explicit directions to a large group returning to visit Kaningarra. Kaningarra is the Walmajarri name for Godfrey's Tank, named in the Christmas Creek manager's letter to the police; it is near Well Forty-seven on the Canning Stock Route. This was the first time Limerick had returned since being forcibly removed fifty-one years earlier.[16]

CHAPTER FIVE WELFARE LAW, WET SEASON LAW

The DNW did not exercise the close level of control over the lives of individuals on the northern stations as they did over the wards of state and inmates of institutions like Moore River in the south of Western Australia. In effect, they assumed that Aboriginal people were the responsibility of the owners of the stations where they lived, and with their limited budget and resources the DNW exercised a light touch.

While occasional incidents and events such as the Leopold walk off and the Warri affair prompted a burst of correspondence, the vast bulk of the material in the relevant files of DNW in the first half of the 1900s is about raising revenue from the stations.

Each station had to obtain a permit to employ natives, and was obliged to make annual payments to the Natives Medical Fund on a 'per head' basis, which in the 1930s was one pound per worker. There is seemingly endless correspondence back and forth between the Commissioner and station managers or Perth head offices regarding overdue payments and haggling over numbers of people and amounts owing. In a typical example, the Christmas Creek file contains a chain of letters and file notes over a fifteen-month period in 1938–39 over a disputed five pounds; at one stage the Deputy Commissioner writes to the head office of the owners, the Emanuel brothers:

> *With reference to the suggestion that if the Department still continues to press for the amendment of the permit and Medical Fund contribution, arrangements should be made for a transfer of all spare natives not wanted by the station to the ration camp at Fitzroy, I would advise that the adoption of this attitude by the Manager is most regrettable and not likely to assist in clearing up any misunderstanding which he chooses to think exists.*[1]

Emanuel brothers eventually coughed up the five pounds, but within months were again in dispute with the Department, refusing to pay a carrier's bill of two pounds for transporting a woman to the Derby Native Hospital, on the grounds that they had paid their contribution to the Medical Fund. But the DNW was adamant, citing legislation requiring pastoralists to 'provide free transport for the [sick] native and send him to the nearest and most accessible hospital'.[2] The file does not record how this matter was resolved.

Other files show very occasional claims by or reimbursements to stations under the Medical Fund. But unless the Fund was also used for other medical purposes, such as directly subsidising the Derby Native Hospital, it seems to have been primarily a revenue-raising mechanism for the Department.

A number of the DNW files for stations in the Fitzroy Valley are begun in 1938. The government station at Moola Bulla seems to represent the Department in the area, with much of the file material channelled through there. Some stations supply lists of Aboriginal people. 'On GO GO Station September 1938' lists seventy-five people, under the categories of 'Married—Buck, Married—Gins, Single, Kids and Useless'.[3] The first list for Brooking Springs details 'all natives and half-castes employed

On GO GO Station September 1938.

Married.

Buck
Saturday @ Jenunga
Tiger @ Lindarrie
Cher Paddy @ Limaroor
Fat Paddy @ Timarria
Long Dave @ Dibbie
No Good Billy
Tommy @ Nulga
Hansen @ Muranga
Jong @ Muliambi
Toby @ Kocatea
Willie @ Mullamilla
Tim Murray @ Ulyanga
Junkabine @ Kamarrung
Padylynch @ Cabilya
Barrie @ Wambi
Long Joe @ Wambi

17.

Gins
Millie @ Willilam
Daisie @ Webie
Mag @ Wickarroo
Anny @ Tanbaria
Medlean @ XXXXXXXXX Munganer
Agnes Bessie @ Minmaria
Lunger @ Minbul
Jumbung @ Badaria
Mary Ann @ Kangaella
Lilly @ Jizuberry
Poddy @ Wgoolgie
Polly @ Gongaring
Daisy @ Tanbaria
Bessie @ Dingana
Gilipsie @ Gongarung
Winnie

16

__SINGLE__

Bob @ Millaloor
Jubiter @ Jubiter
David @ Boorwarie
Monkey @ Jababee
Drone @ Mungunga
Peter @ Mugibray
Jack @ Yumagi
Possum @ Pugani
Charlie @ Wirrni
Brumby @ Millaloor
Big Brumby @ Candallon
Sing Poo @ Billawilli
Dutchie @ Angin
Podgey

14

__KIDS.__

Mick @ Dibbie
Terry @ Malaby
Alick @ Jugoodun
Sammy @ Kaminga
June @ Nungmarie
Abe @ Wingarrie
Norah @ Yarraroor
Ruby @ Jillawillie
George @ Limarra
Rohda @ Mirrando
Mosey

11

__USELESS__

Go Go Billy @ Karringi
Nola @ Yagoolar
Judy @ Lingadie
Jinny @ Gingullie
Blind Duncan @ Mayilla
Old Lilly @ Neddie
Yarry @ Iola
Blind Charlie @ Togadagina
Sing Poo Mother @ Yanmaria
Rosie @ Jugae
Annie @ Bidparra
Lime Stone Billy @ June
Blind Maggie
Jongs Mother @ Dinga
Saturday's Mother @ Mullinga
Rosy @ Yumberrina
Nellie @ Milharia
Mad Nuggett.

18..

18

18.

List of Aboriginal people, Go Go Station 1938

here', listing twenty-two males under the headings of 'Boys, Children and Half-Castes', prompting immediate demands from the DNW for increased permit and medical fund payments.[4]

Throughout these years, however, the files contain very few references to conditions on the stations, and no discussions at all about the welfare of the people, despite the Department's name.

The open brutality of what Ginger Nganawilla called 'the early days' gradually reduced. But the environment on the stations remained harsh. Some station owners felt a responsibility to 'their natives', and provided better rations or more frequent issues of clothing than was normal. But through to at least the Second World War the status quo remained. No wages were paid. No education was provided for children. Health care was virtually non-existent, with regular flu epidemics taking their toll of the old and weak. On many stations no accommodation was provided, and people lived in camps of cobbled together humpies. The 'gold standard', that started to appear on some stations from the 1950s, was a square, one-room hut of corrugated iron with an earth floor.

And it was all underpinned by the 'code' Biskup described; an attitude that the natives belonged to the station. The language of the police and the bureaucrats still spoke of absconders and indigents, raids and runaways. And short of leaving their country and their familiar world altogether, the people had no real choices; it was a station camp, or the police ration camp, where the police were only interested in moving them back out to the stations.

It was a code and a system only two or three steps removed from slavery. People were not individually bought and sold, but their freedom of movement and their right to choose where to live and work were severely restricted. They could be—and were—arbitrarily removed from their place of residence. At times their children were summarily taken from them, never to be seen again. The station owners did not legally own their Aboriginal workforce. But in effect, through the provisions of the Aborigines Act, and its permit system administered by the DNW, they leased their workers from the government, and then worked, housed and paid them like slaves.

For all its harshness, there was another side to life on the stations. The managers were interested in little beyond satisfying their labour needs, and with few exceptions were completely uninterested in the lives of the Kimberley people. Apart from the odd police patrol, and even rarer visit from the DNW, people were largely left to their own devices. Once a station's demands had been met, and within the limits and constraints of the time, each station community was largely autonomous and independent, subject to minimal outside interference.

Sandy Cox remembers that:

> *Station people used to walk to another station, you know, they used to walk from Christmas Creek to Noonkanbah, from Noonkanbah to Jubilee, you know, Cherrabun and all that place, they used to walk around close country, you know, to meet blokes, they bin for ceremony, you know, kids.*

June Davis recalls it this way:

> *They bin have their law on the station. They always travel everywhere. They go right up to Tablelands, Lansdowne, Bedford. All around they would walk. Just by foot. Right up to Mount House. They bin walk all round. Brooking Spring.*

> *Noonkanbah. The whole Fitzroy Valley area. They would go right up Louisa. Right through to Halls Creek. Just by foot. They bin go everywhere.*
>
> *Like in those days it happened every year—like a holiday time. Just for a short time and then people go back to their station. They bin chuck out their narga* and put their trousers and shirt, dresses on and go back and work for kartiya and do that year in, year out.*

People were free to maintain their culture, language and traditions. The time when this freedom really came into play was the annual wet season holiday time. As the Wet approached, the relentless cycle of station work wound down, the managers would head into Derby to board ship for their passage to a holiday down in Perth, and the workers were released for a month or two.

Sandy Cox describes how it worked:

> *When they finished stock at season time they used to take their boots off, shirt and trousers, leave them back in the store. Put them back inside. They used to give them just narga. Get a stick of tobacco, tea leaf, might be, mixed with sugar, just a little bit, about that much, and half a bag of flour, or not half a bag of flour but put it in a bag, or something, little bag, little bag and he last a couple of days, that's all. After the season come back to work.*

---

* 'Kartiya' is a common term among Kimberley people to refer to whitefellas.

It was known as 'walkabout' time, and for good reason. People walked vast distances. There was leisure time for hunting and fishing, and catching up with friends and relations from other stations. But above all, it was law time. People would gather for the ceremonies that kept the law and culture alive. Boys were initiated to become men. Marriages were arranged. The spiritual fabric of life remained strong.

Torrential rain and raging rivers were no deterrent. Kevin Oscar tells of one wet season adventure:

> *We went down to Muludja, we crossed the river empty. They had some dancing there, then couple of days later we bin come back, we bin find the river full bank to bank, dark too night time ... We got all the logs together, tied up all the logs. There used to be an old fence the other side of Bungardi, the old bullock paddock for Go Go. We bin take out all the wire from there. Take em wire, cut up the log, tied up all the logs, like that.*
>
> *I was sitting on one of them there. Darkest night, sitting on them logs, floating across the Fitzroy river, lightning flicking. One bloke swam for that tree down up there, he swim to that tree and tie the wire from that tree, well that whole thing just drift around like that. And the other old bloke he'd swim over there and tie that up to tree and we cut across the river like that.*

The Walmajarri of the desert exodus walked the country south of the Fitzroy. The Gooniyandi of Louisa Downs would walk north through the O'Donnell Ranges to meet up with the Kija people of Tablelands Station. The Bunuba from Leopold and Brooking would walk as far as Napier Downs and back, or north to Mornington and Glenroy. And people from these stations would

Kevin Oscar

make their way into the Fitzroy Valley country. Peoples who would have been strangers in the old world before the stations took over, shared stories, knowledge and ceremonies.

Politically and economically the peoples of the Fitzroy Valley were completely subjugated. But they maintained a rich cultural and spiritual life.

CHAPTER SIX THE FIRST WINDS OF CHANGE

In 1942 Broome was bombed by the Japanese, with heavy loss of life. Most of the dead were Dutch refugees who had just escaped from the Japanese invasion of Dutch East Indies, and were caught in boats and seaplanes moored on the harbour. But away from Broome itself the Second World War had little impact on the existing patterns of life in the Kimberley. An air force base was established on Noonkanbah Station, 90 kilometres west of Fitzroy Crossing, but it seems to have been self-contained, with little interaction with the local population.

But the year after the war finished, events in the Pilbara sent a shiver of apprehension through both pastoralists and the authorities. On May Day 1946, most of the Aboriginal workforce on the stations of the Pilbara went on strike. The authorities hit back hard, with many of the strike leaders repeatedly jailed. The dispute dragged on. Some improvements to the token wages that were already being paid in the Pilbara were won. But many of the strikers never went back to the stations, and formed an independent community, making a living by prospecting and harvesting pearl shell.[1]

Wages were starting to be an issue of discussion in the Kimberley. One police officer's patrol journal for 1946 records discussions with the managers of Upper Liveringa and Noonkanbah on 3 and 4 May, just as the Pilbara strike was getting underway. The manager, Mr Rose, at Upper Liveringa, he wrote, 'is suffering a severe shortage of native labour' and 'has done all in his power short of offering wages in cash ... Mr Rose is of the opinion that the time has arrived at Liveringa when the changeover from the old system of wages in kind will have to be replaced by cash payments and or the introduction of white labour'. His stated reason for not doing so is 'that it would upset the labour situation on neighbouring stations'.[2]

At Noonkanbah, according to this officer, the manager, Kerwood, 'has a number of half castes employed who are paid wages in cash but the station natives still receive food, clothes and tobacco as in the past ... and [Kerwood] is not favourable to a changeover as he is of the opinion that the station natives are happier and more contented under the present system'. Yet the policeman also says that 'a change over to payments in cash would not solve the problem as other stations would be forced to follow suit and any natives [the manager] had attracted to Upper Liveringa by such payments would then return to the original station from whence they came'.[3] It would seem that the unpaid workers were not happy and contented enough to stay where they were if there was a prospect of getting paid elsewhere, and from around this time, reports and discussions about wages and their implications become very common in the DNW files.

Until the 1940s, apart from a very occasional tour by someone from head office, all the field work for the DNW was done by the police. In 1949 a new district officer, with previous experience as a patrol officer in New Guinea, was appointed to Derby. District Officer Pullen was an enthusiastic and diligent officer, and a prolific report writer. He was no radical, but was a zealous reformer, who seemed to introduce an entirely new approach and way of thinking to the work of the Department. His first annual report, written after three months, was published in the *West Australian*.

> *From headquarter's records … I had learnt that the general conditions of native workers and their dependants in the West Kimberley were not considered good … Many* [Derby townspeople] *spoke scathingly of shocking conditions, cheap labour and the curse of absentee owners … Antagonism to the introduction of new blood into native affairs grew much less because the better types in the community quickly appreciated the benefits to be derived from completely dissociating native affairs from the police. People are unanimous about the wisdom of this …*[4]

He talks of 'well rehearsed opinions that the natives should not be interfered with', claims 'that money would spoil them', and then observes:

> *Also I had been led to believe that the stations were, great-heartedly, maintaining hundreds of aged and indigent people. My first patrol through the Kimberleys debunked this latter idea rather completely. I found that only 72 indigents were being fed, scattered over 12 stations, that is six a station.*[5]

Pullen advocated housing schemes and minimum standards. He advocated the establishment of an education and pastoral training institution in Fitzroy Crossing, but the real hot issue was wages. In the summary of his first major patrol in 1949, under the heading of 'Wages For Native Workers', he writes that among the managers:

> *It was unanimously agreed that the payment of wages was inevitable. To put them at ease, I told them that, personally, I thought it would be unwise to suddenly raise natives from nothing … to fantastic rates. They should not forget, however,*

> *that there were many people who thought quite differently and who were prepared to agitate for award rates for natives in every industry. I already had evidence of an active attempt to recruit natives to the ranks of the A.W.U.* [Australian Workers Union]. *This was not a crime but it was definitely a pointer … I found that some natives are already receiving wages at the rate of 5/- and 10/- per month and all found, and that there are cash hand-outs to drovers.*[6]

The year before, an inquiry had publicised the fact that the Kimberley was the only region in Australia still not paying wages of any kind to Aboriginal station workers, and recommendations had been made for the immediate introduction of a nominal cash wage. The Pastoralists Association, the body which represented pastoralists throughout the state, including still at this time many of the famous pioneering families of the Western Australian establishment, had objected to this as 'unsuited to the present development of the natives in the Kimberleys'.[7]

Pullen was clearly a believer in the introduction of wages, and his reports are full of references to discussions of the matter with owners and managers. The DNW Commissioner writes to him in August 1949 that:

> *I have discussed the matter of wages payments in the Kimberley Districts with the Hon. Minister* [for Native Welfare], *and it is his intention to meet the representatives of the pastoralists in Perth in the near future for another discussion on the matter, at which I hope a degree of finality will be reached.*[8]

Pullen's lengthy reports were circulated around the public service for comment. Some of the responses reveal that the senior bureaucrats were still very much of the 'smooth the dying pillow' school of thought. The Assistant Commissioner of Public Health writes:

> *I have difficulty in understanding your concern over the falling native birthrate. Surely it were better not to be born at all than to be borne into the conditions we seek to ameliorate ... I think your falling birthrate is a natural withdrawal and decline of a primitive race confronted with the hazards and responsibilities of civilisation.*[9]

It is also clear, for the first time in any of the DNW files sighted, that Pullen actively engaged the Aboriginal people on the stations, seeking their opinions, and at times complaints. On another patrol later in 1949 he wrote:

> *There is no doubt at all that the natives themselves want wages and that this demand will continue to grow in strength ... Most of them are already 'wages conscious' but don't know how to outwardly express their views. They are not encouraged to do so on the stations and any white man who mentions wages in the vicinity of a station is branded a Communist ... The aboriginal appears to be a most discerning bloke and he knows that something is in the air and stoically awaits results ... And he is shrewd enough to realise that he is a pretty important unit in the community and not easily discarded.*[10]

And on his next patrol in September:

> *Managers say:– 'My natives are contented, they get everything they want.' But they have simply made themselves believe this by a constant telling of the story to anyone ready to listen. But the*

only people they haven't asked for a confirmation of the claim are the natives themselves. This occurred to me when I saw a dozen adult male natives at Go Go Station walking away like 'Kordies' (dull, mechanical men) after they had received their midday meal—1 round of dry bread and 1 mug of black tea. Recently I read of a very similar diet being issued to the inmates of an internment camp in Siberia—the only difference being that the bread over there was black.[11]

On this patrol Pullen visited Brooking Gorge, and strongly urged that it be made the site of the school he was agitating for, advising that the Brooking Springs Station management had no objections. He also notes the first instance seen in the files of a citizenship application, from Frank Hunter who was working as a mechanic and handyman at the Crossing Inn. The application was supported by DNW and granted.

By November 1949 it seems that the talks in Perth had resulted in concrete proposals, with the station managers having received copies of the submission made by the Pastoralists Association. Pullen notes that 'Quanbun (G.C. Rose) thought that the rates suggested could not be lower'.[12] He continued:

Stations that are influenced by Messrs Mawley & Forrest naturally parrot their views—it would seem that these two gentlemen are still living in the age of 10 to 15 years ago and are, unfortunately, telling a good tale to the Pastoralists in Perth.

The actual set-up on the stations is that about 1/3 of the workers are intelligent blokes and excellent stockmen—they they have been handling money at race meetings and on droving trips for

THE COMMISSIONER OF NATIVE AFFAIRS.

Patrol Report 1 - 49/50.

Very many thanks f or loan of above report. I read it with particular interest having just returned from a 5 weeks' tour of the North West, where I had the good fortune to meet Mr. Elliot-Smith and Mr. Pullen.

From Mr. Pullen's account of native living conditions, I thought at first glance that they must all be living in one of our Northern Hotels. The fact is that the native position must be viewed against the broader background of the conditions under which the white population itself is content to live. Where we have men raising thousands of head of cattle and content themselves to live on tinned margarine and dried milk and reside in tin shacks we can expect little from them of appreciation for better conditions for natives.

I have difficulty in understanding your concern over the falling native birthrate. Surely it were better not to be born at all than to be born into the conditions we seek to ameliorate.

I do not think that vitamin deficiency plays any great part in this lack of fertility. India and China have lived on the brink of starvation for generations and still their countless millions multiply.

With the one exception of New Zealand, a rise in the standard of living in the Nations of the World is concommittant with a declining birth rate. On the other hand, the prevalence of sore eyes is strongly suggestive of vitamin deficiency. The deficiency lies in the absence of the basic foods - fresh milk, fresh butter and eggs from the diet. In a cattle raising country such a deficiency is an indication of pure laziness and nothing more. I may say that goat's milk and dried milk are poor substitutes for cow's milk as regards vitamins.

I think your falling birthrate is a natural withdrawal and decline of a primitive race confronted with the hazards and responsibilities of civilisation, aided considerably by the playful native passtime of urethrotomy or "whistle cocking." That the native remains still in such numbers in the North, is an indication of how little has yet been felt of the impact of civilisation in that area.

I, in company with all humanitarians, advocate wages and better conditions for the native; but the higher the wages and the better the conditions, the sooner the white man will be able to compete with him on the stations and the sooner his race will disappear.

We are very much aware that a land operation is the only method of bringing effective medical care and supervision to the hinterland. That and a better Flying Doctor Service is under discussion, our only real difficulty is to get the doctors and here we are exerting every ingenuity.

We are in communication with the Police Commissioner at present regarding the possibility of a round up of natives - bush and station - from Le Grange to Wallal, for medical inspection. This is at the request of station owners in that area, perturbed at the occurrences of one or two cases of leprosy in their areas. This operation to be successful should take place before the rains at the end of October.

We would be grateful for any help or suggestions you can offer in this undertaking.

27 SEP 1949

D.AW
23.9.49.

ASSISTANT COMMISSIONER OF PUBLIC HEALTH.

Comment on a West Kimberley patrol officer's report by Assistant Commissioner of Public Health

years. A third are not quite so bright and the remaining third, on some stations, might be classed as 'munjongs' or 'bushmen' in New Guinea parlance.

Therefore the idea behind Condition 24 was that, knowing that these grades existed, so would they be classified so far as wages were concerned. To deny 2/3 of the workers some monetary reward for their services by quoting and enlarging on the lack of intelligence and gullibility of the remaining third bushmen, savours of straightout deception ...

It will be noted that complaints were more numerous on this patrol and the particular one by MICK [sic] *of Jubilee Downs Station indicates 'the writing on the wall'. 'Would it be O.K. if we left this station to go to a station where wages were being paid and conditions better' ...*

The Mawley-Forrest group are fighting a losing battle and I anticipate that on each successive patrol, the blackfellows will ask more questions about wages and, sooner or later, they will have to be told the truth.

I have reported honestly what managers and owners have said to me—what they say to their superiors might be different—like the blackfellow, they might feel that they should answer their employer as their employer would like them to answer. But I don't think it really matters. The blackfellows will solve it themselves, but, it is to be hoped, in a nice way.[13]

Despite the tone of frustration, the same report says that some stations have already started to pay wages, and others are planning to do so in the near future. He also reports on the beginnings of improvements to housing at some stations, and plans at Go Go and Christmas Creek stations to establish schools.

In 1950 a voluntary agreement was reached with the Pastoralists Association, for payment of one pound per month to stockmen, and ten shillings per month for domestics. This rate of one pound per month compared to the Western Australian male basic wage in 1950 of eight pounds and fifteen shillings per week, or approximately thirty-five pounds a month.[14] Yet Pullen's comments indicate that with 'Condition 24' the pastoralists were using a forerunner of the argument for a 'slow worker' clause that would be run sixteen years later in the Northern Territory to further reduce any costs they might face.

The Louisa Downs Station file contains ledgers drawn up by the manager recording his payments. The first of these records wages for the two months to 31 August 1950. Thirteen 'stock boys' are employed, with seven of them receiving two pounds, i.e. the recommended pound per month, three receiving one pound, and three receiving ten shillings. Twelve 'females' are employed, with nine of them receiving one pound, and three receiving ten shillings.[15]

These figures would seem to reflect the three-tier structure described above by Pullen, with a slow-worker clause of some kind included. But on Louisa at least, most of the men are on the top tier, rather than the 'deception' he describes of placing the majority on the lowest rate. This low rate of five shillings per month amounted to approximately a shilling (ten cents) a week, which is less than one per cent of the basic wage at this time of eight pounds fifteen.

CHAPTER SEVEN THE GOOD OLD DAYS

Good old days. Yeah. Everybody talk about the 'good old days'. Well back in that time, because, as everybody saying, back in the good old days, it was the good old days, even though people lived under the authority of those people, you know.

Topsy Chestnut

Mervyn Street, an artist who lives at Muludja and Yiyili communities, created a wonderful mural that adorned the walls of Tarunda Supermarket in Fitzroy Crossing, until the building burnt down in 2009. The mural included a depiction of the people in the old days travelling into Fitzroy Crossing for the races.

The people had a good time meeting people at races time. They used to go with the tractor in the race. We fellas from Louisa we had to come in a semi-trailer truck and that's the only way to get into Fitzroy and Halls Creek, riding on those truck, get in the race. But not safe for riding on the truck, like there was a drum tied up to the rope, dangerous thing, but we had to get down to the races.

Mervyn Street

Eat in or Take - Away
Ph: 9191 5031

Mervyn Street's mural on Tarunda supermarket walls.
The supermarket was burned to the ground in 2009.

The Fitzroy races of 1950 would have been the first time that most of the Aboriginal people there had money in their pockets. District Officer Pullen was also at the races that year, and reported extensively.

> *Congregation of Natives: Between the 31st August and 2nd September, 500 or more natives, in family groups, were congregated at Fitzroy Crossing. Race time is now regarded as their principal holiday time, when they foregather to renew old acquaintances, entertain and enjoy the racing and sporting events.*
>
> *Sept. 1st was partly devoted to natives sports and I was able to assist the Committee considerably by rounding up entrants for the natives events. And they responded very well. There were flat races, in heats, for adult males and females, for young girls and boys and for the tiny tots. Prizes were handed out freely and the races created considerable hilarity amongst blacks and whites.*
>
> *Old hands told me that it was the largest collection of natives seen for many years. Another aspect was that they were all 'holding'. I actually witnessed the August payment of natives from Jubilee, Cherrabun and Christmas Creek Stations. Trade boomed in the local store ... Dress materials were in great demand so that the women, perhaps for the first time, participated in the spending feast. They appeared to be careful buyers and thought hard and long before committing themselves to a purchase—one Manager told me that he thought the payment of wages was contributing to the emancipation of the women—they no longer felt so completely dependent on the whims of their menfolk.*

> *Native Labour: It was certain that with such a gathering of natives, employed by 15 different stations, there would be some disputes between Owners and Managers—an inevitable aftermath of a race meeting. So it was that I had to arbitrate in a number of cases immediately after the races had ended.*
>
> *A native from Go Go wished to go to Fossil Downs—one from Fossil Downs wished to work at The Springs—two women from The Springs desired a change of climate to Ellendale and a Springs native had a hankering to go to Jubilee.*
>
> *In each case I gathered together the owners and the natives but I found that the idea that a native is still bound body and soul to a particular Station dies hard that allowing free movement will damn the whole country. But actually, the fact that there were only the movements abovementioned after such a large meeting of natives suggests that the employees are not yet steeped in revolutionary ideas and are remaining rather loyal to their old employers.*[1]

District Officer Pullen seems to disappear from the Derby office not long after this, with no further trace of him in the files. It would be twenty-five years until an officer with similar energy and enthusiasm appeared again.

The 1950s is the decade in which many of today's elders and leaders grew up, when most of their memories begin. It was perhaps the most stable decade in the history of the Kimberley since the arrival of the whitefellas. Australia was 'riding on the sheep's back', and the vast sheep stations of the West Kimberley hitched a ride. For the cattle stations the meatworks in Wyndham, Derby and Broome provided a secure market and accessible outlets, and each season the drovers pushed the mobs of cattle to these works along the network of stock routes that crisscrossed the Kimberley.

The frontier wars of the 1890s were two generations in the past. The worst excesses of the 'early days' had abated. All workers were receiving payment of some kind, though for many it would disappear in 'book-up'* at the station store. Each station community was by now relatively stable. But this is not to say that it was an easy life, as Mervyn Street recounts:

> *Taking my memory back, right back to station time, right back to Louisa, I'm really living rough life there. Old people was working hard just say from sunrise until it's dark and then, after holiday come, they had no decent house. They just living in a tent, everybody was living in a tent. Cutting up the leaves and putting on the canvas, and no lights inside. There was only a fire there and just sleeping inside and the thing about Louisa old camp, down there old reserve, people just walk down with a billy can and getting water from soak, and hanging up there, and the water hanging up in the trees there, and when that water get dry you got to walk down again and you gotta use that water for boiling your tea and wash your clothes and all that kind now. Go nice and clean, go and work for station and back again and people had no washing machine or anything in the camp you know. People had no tap to boil the tea on. They just go get soak water.*
>
> *I know all that life, well now I seen it through and that's when I telling a story you know, for myself, you know because rough time*

* *'Killer' is the term used for a station beast slaughtered and butchered for local consumption.*

> *for me and looking at the old people they had a rough life and all that time they work for nothing.*

Hunger stays in the memory. Even on Fossil Downs, which had a reputation that was probably the best in the Kimberley for its treatment of its workers, this was an issue, as Mervyn's wife June Davis tells:

> *Our old people bin tell us, 'We bin have biggest starve at la* [sic] *station, and we used to go around then stealing anything, you know, tomato, pawpaw, grapefruit.' And they always tell us, 'Don't go to that garden, kartiya might hunt em out you fellas. Don't go in there. Don't go stealing anything.' But we used to go there every day in the morning before all the gardeners used to go along there you know.*

Sandy Cox grew up at Christmas Creek and Go Go:

> *They used to get fed through the window, one piece of bread, that's all. No meat. Sometimes they'd get killer* but they used to chop it into little piece, get bread, one piece of bread and a bit of meat on top of that and that's it. That's to last him all day. And then might be for supper, same thing.*

Jean Cox was at Go Go:

> *When I bin work in the station, I used to get rations like tea, sugar, flour only with a small bag. It's Sunday, but they'll be right through next week, 'Right. Here's your ration.' Get two bags through the* [store] *window, tea, sugar.*

---

* *'Killer' is the term used for a station beast slaughtered and butchered for local consumption.*

Meagre rations were one thing, but the attitude of some station staff added to the indignity, as Annette Kogolo describes the set-up at Go Go:

> *And they never used to just pass it, they used to throw it through the window, you gotta bin try and catch it.*

And Stella Jimbidie tells a similar tale of Cherrabun:

> *We bin have one manager, rough one at Djugerari* [new Cherrabun]. *He bin throw em all that tea leaf, sugar,* [on the] *ground, we bin pick em up.*

In 1961 a Go Go resident of unspecified age, but apparently an adult, was admitted to the hospital in Fitzroy Crossing suffering from malnutrition. A DNW Welfare Inspector wrote:

> *Enquiries were made on a tour of the Station with respect to this case. It is quite apparent that the trouble stems from the lack of vegetables and fruit, the staple diet consisting of meat and bread in the main. In fact all cases of yaws and sores would appear to be caused by lack of nutritious commodities in the daily diet. Any of the latter items can only be bought from the store. The wages paid to employees is only a pittance, hence the purchase of extras is impossible.*[2]

At the most fundamental levels, station management continued to control the lives and affairs of people in the camps, and to do so capriciously. Kevin Oscar tells stories from his childhood in the 1950s and '60s of what could happen if a manager thought there were too many dogs in a camp:

Jean Cox

> *They used to get the policemen to shoot all the dogs at the station. They go to Brooking, Leopold, shoot em all the dog. Come to black fella camp, shoot all the dogs. Some old girl used to get that word, 'Ah policeman coming.' They'd hide, take over and hide all the dogs. Whatever dog left round the camp, bang, bang, bang, bang, they shoot them, bang, bang. In front of the people. In front of them!*
>
> *The people see their dogs dead, they pack their gear and they go. People just move out. Walk away. Sometimes they'd just go along the river and stay there for a few weeks, til they settled down. The manager used to go look for them, or policemen go look for them, take em back.*

Among the most recent arrivals to station country, the desert people, fear of the whitefellas was still deeply ingrained. Olive Knight, who was born in 1946, tells this story that must have taken place in the early 1950s. She has written a Walmajarri account of the story in *Out of the Desert*:[3]

> *It's called the 'White Strangers' where these people, I can clearly remember as a child how they were passing through Chestnut Bore because that was the main highway through here up to Hall's Creek and my Father was such a brave desert man and he was my step-Father, well not my real Father, my step-Father but he was a wonderful person and I remember him walking up to these white strangers and meeting them and greeting them and they in exchange thought, 'Well he's a friendly old man.' And they gave him rations of tin meat and tobacco. But the women were cowering in the background, in their tents and they were always they had all sorts of ulterior motives like thoughts that these men were*

coming to skin us alive and all this sort of thing. And we as kids were listening to these women. We saw knives all right. And this old woman, Auntie I called her, one of the Jubadah family, and she said that night, 'Now give me those tins of meat and tobacco, I want to chuck it all away because they all poison that lot. And besides I saw something shine there glint of a knife they going to skin us alive tonight.'

Oh. And then they took off into the night. It was pitch black and the old people carrying us on their backs and running into the bush. And we stayed there until the next day and maybe the kartiyas they was looking for us, wondering where we had gone. And they went away. Oh dear me it was quite funny, when you look back at it.

And being poisoned was still very fresh in our minds because we'd heard of people being poisoned. So you didn't risk anything. Even the tins were. We couldn't eat the tin foods. We thought they were poisoned too.

Although people still have a fund of stories along these lines, of rough managers, insensitive police and the like, there is no doubt that from today's perspective, most of the people old enough to remember look back on this time with a degree of fondness and nostalgia; even as 'the good old days'.

Some of this sentiment is the almost universal nostalgia for the more carefree times of childhood.

Olive Knight's 'White Strangers' story above is from her early years at Chestnut Bore.

> *I came down as a child from Bohemia Downs, up this way, and then lived here in Christmas Creek for a while and then lived most of my childhood at Chestnut Bore which is now kind of close to Ngalingkadji [a contemporary outstation community].*

> *There was a little outstation for Christmas Creek. They had a man there caretaking the outstation. But it more or less look like a station in every which way because it had tanks and a garage and then there was a huge kitchen there if I can remember it. Then there were goats the women would milk. The women would milk and make butter and all that sort of thing and I can recall there was an orange grove there. We used to pick the oranges ripening in the tree.*

Topsy Chestnut, who now lives at Ngalingkadji, also grew up at Chestnut Bore.

> *We had one white bloke there, running it. It was right on the main highway, the main highway that was going to Halls Creek. All the traffic used to come through there. Quite a few families were living there with just that one white man. We were just our own little community.*

> *That little place was just like a little roadhouse kind of thing, you know. And all them old people used to work there. My Mother used to cook and things and we used to serve those tourists that used to come through there. You know. Tourists that were going around*

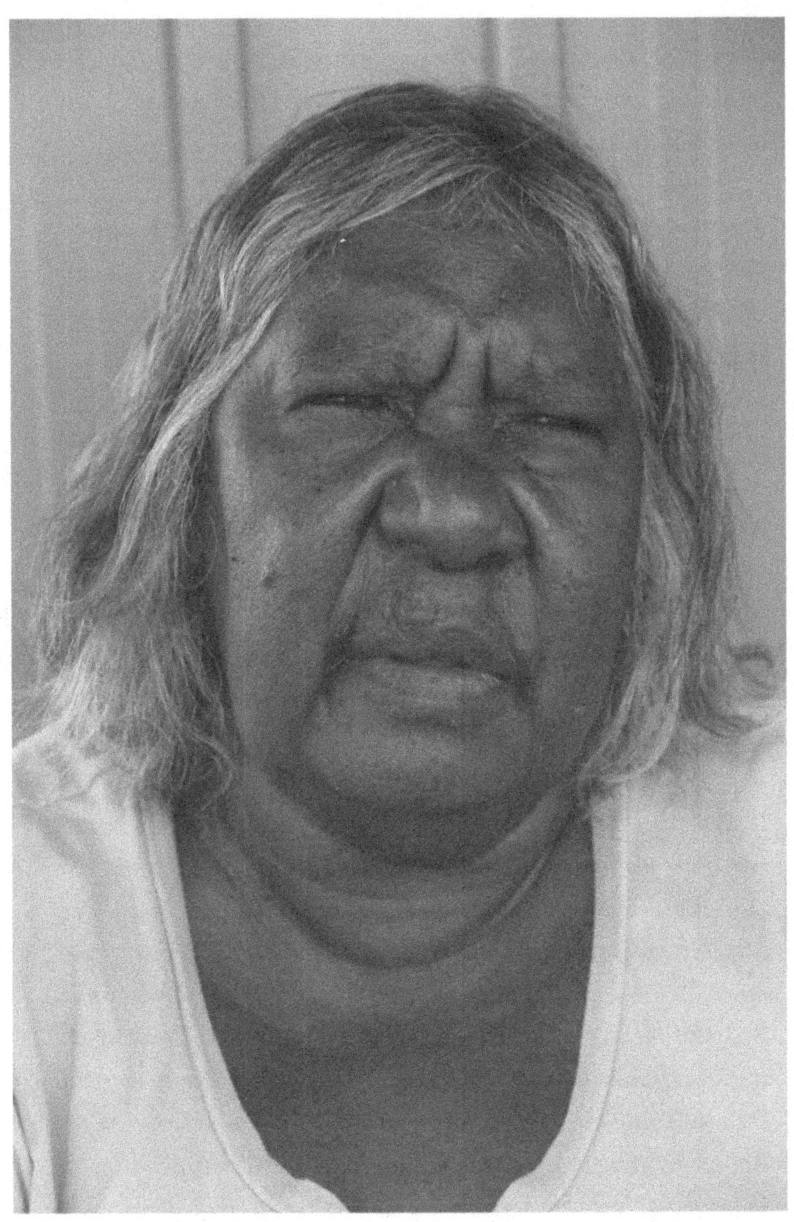

Topsy Chestnut

the road. The old people used to serve them with fresh fruit, vegies and bread and stuff like that, you know, and fresh goat milk and thing like that.

Main thing was just; this white man we had from Go Go he was, that place was outstation for Go Go, his job was to go out and check all the bores, and the old people used to go out with him to check bores along this area you know.

No school, no nothing. Just the old people working there. We just went and played round there. We just went out playing on, everywhere there, just we did nothing.

June Davis grew up on Fossil Downs Station. Since the 1880s it had been run by the McDonald family, who had become the aristocrats of the Kimberley pastoral industry. It had a grand homestead by Kimberley standards, and had hosted a visit from a governor general.

It was just home to us. We didn't worry about the big house. We didn't worry about the governor coming out or anything like that. It never occurred to us that it was very important that place. Mrs McDonald was a model in her early days before she was married. We didn't think of that. We just saw her as, like she was a second mother to us. She raised us, fed us and all that at the station. It was good but, you know, I was just wondering now why she was doing that for us. You know? Like when we were on the station growing up, we used to go up, Mrs Mac used to oh bring the kids up and have tea here. We'll give them soup-soup.

June Davis

You know we led a healthy life. None of the old people were sick. Like us kids we bin getting sick. She must have want to take us in to feed us up and we had to live a healthy life as well. But to me, oh this is home. We could go anywhere. Just go to the big house with our parents and see what they doing and we'd just go stickybeak in the office and all that. 'Oh just go oh this is nice.' But we didn't care about picking up anything or taking it home with us. We just wandered around the homestead or followed our family where they working and all that.

I used to sit with Dad in the garage and just watch what he was doing. Why did he fix cars for kartiyas? I used to just sit there for hours and Dad used to tell me, 'You go home love. Go to Mother. Go play with the kids.'

'No I want to stay here and watch you.'

'No. Look. You go back to Mother.'

And sometimes they used to tell us, 'Just go bush. Go down the creek. Go spring. Go play.' Old Mrs Mac and sometimes [her daughter] *Merrilee used to just load us up on that biggest jeep and take us down here where they bin have that garden down here and we could feed the chooks and everything. Chase all their chooks and make them mad there. She didn't care. She used to love having us.*

Stella Jimbidie grew up on Cherrabun Station, first at Old Cherrabun on the river, near today's Yakanarra Community, then at New Cherrabun, or Djugareri.

Stella Jimbidie

I bin born in Old Cherrabun. We bin born in Old Cherrabun station. We didn't go to school. We bin grown up, all the family bin look after us, and we bin working, you know, same time gotta parents and so bin learnin' us work, how to work.

We bin go nanny goat, put nanny goat in yard, help em morning time, they bin take us, all the parents, Aunty, Granny, and the old people bin work there, sweeping, outside front. Outside, outside la [sic] *fence, pull em out all the grass, and plants, sweep im, not got a kartiya broom they bin sweep em with, bush broom. That manager bin like im that bush broom, clean im round, all round.*

Cooking tea, this big boiler, for everybody, breakfast, dinner, they bin cooking and they bin take us swimming, all day swimming all the kids. Swimming, swimming everyday and they bin give us work, working now, working there in kitchen, plate, wash im, plate wash im, helpin' missus.

And we didn't get any money yet. Not yet. No money. Only for free, free clothes, free tucker from the store, every Sunday. Sunday or Saturday, I forget now.

Then we bin grow up more bigger and learning, they bin learning us cooking, bread-making, yeast, for bread, finish, and we bin shipped out now. That old Harry Scriviner say, 'You mob can't stay here, too much big flood coming up. I'll shift em you mob like Djugareri, other side, more better.'

> *We didn't go to school. Missionary bin come with truck for school, we bin go big mob for the Jubilee mob, some from Quanbun, some from Noonkanbah, they bin come this way and when we bin go back that way, Cherrabun, that manager never let um us. He bin keep all fella for work.*

Joe Brown recalls it as a simpler time:

> *Well we bin like station because we had a good life in the work line you know. We start mustering cattle, we bin like that life because we bin working together, you know, like people had like team you know. All the workers used to have station had stock camp with their team and yard builders had their team and all the fence builders, they had a team you know. Good things been happening to the people and that's why people get round very well, you know. Never worrying about to get away you know. They was just doing their job. That's what they living. Didn't think what next gonna come you know.*

Topsy Chestnut is more reflective:

> *We lived under the authority of them, you know, that's why everybody saying I suppose 'back in the good old days' because it was nice and free, you know they were free to go here and there, everything, fishing, hunting, and things like even though they didn't realise the land was theirs, you know. People didn't realise the land was theirs.*

Because right from the start this kartiyas had us under control you know, had our people under control and no matter how they were under the control of the kartiyas, they used to, you know, just do as kartiya was telling them to do whatever, you know, but they was happy living there then.

That's why they are saying it's the good old days, even though some people were treated very bad in those days by managers, you know.

CHAPTER EIGHT MISSIONARIES AND CITIZENS

When we bin live on the station, we bin speak our language but when we get into the hostel, mission we never speak our language. That kartiya bin just tell us not to talk in our language. You know we were losing it. And we more or less come back home and sit down with the old people and we bin always ask our parents, I bin always ask my parents, 'What wrong. We don't allowed to talk our language at the Mission?' 'No they going to learn you English now.'

June Davis

The most significant change to the community dynamics in the Fitzroy Valley in the 1950s was the establishment by the DNW in 1950 of 'the Depot', which soon became 'the Mission'. For the first five years this institution struggled; through the mixed motivations over its purpose described in the opening chapter, an ongoing shortage of resources, and through 1953–54, a feud between the two senior missionaries. The highest number of residents in 1951 was thirty-six people.[1] An annual report for 1953 says the 'inmate average has remained at about twenty-five'.[2]

But in 1955 the Mission was put on a much firmer footing in terms of its numbers and government subsidies. Moola Bulla Station, which had been established as a government depot, or ration station, in 1910, and had become an arm of State Government policy and administration, and a dumping ground for 'troublemakers' like Warri, was suddenly closed down and sold off to a private pastoralist.

The DNW 'Register of Inmates' for the Mission shows that on 23 and 25 July 1955, seventy-one people are admitted as inmates, all from Moola Bulla, and in the following days and weeks, more follow. These records are supported by the accounts of two missionaries of the time, Melvina and Nelson Rowley, as told in the book *Moola Bulla: In the Shadow of the Mountain.*[3]

> *We got this message from the government, the Native Affairs Department. Mr Smoker had a phone call to say that the people had been put off Moola Bulla Station, up near Halls Creek, and they were sending them to us ... They said 'We'll send you tents and we'll send you flour and whatever you need.' ... It was only a day or two later when this truck arrived with thirty children on board, and there were four women came with them to look after them ...* [On] *the truck that came a couple of days later, they were on that truck as thick as they could stick. Every available spot was taken up with somebody hanging on, either sitting on the bonnet or on the hood on the top, or else sat in. In those days the truck had those running boards, they used to stand on that. Every available space ... And then they came in dribs and drabs. The man who brought them, he left straight away to come back for*

> *another load ... I think it was over a period of about two weeks, they finally all came in. It was about a hundred and fifty, plus the number that was already there.*[4]

This removal was not a matter of choice. At the whim of the Department these people became 'inmates' of the Mission rather than 'inmates' of Moola Bulla. Most of them had no connection to Fitzroy Crossing; it is just where they were sent, to solve a problem that DNW had. The Rowleys' description of the grossly overcrowded truck bringing powerless refugees to an unknown destination brings to mind District Officer Pullen's parallels in another instance to Siberia.

The future of the Mission was secured. Many of the adults left to find work on the stations, but very many of the children stayed on. And during the second half of the 1950s, increasing numbers of parents on the stations agreed—or were convinced by DNW or the missionaries—to let their children stay in the hostel and go to school.

Through these later years of the 1950s and into the 1960s the numbers at the Mission fluctuated, but never dropped much below 120, and the comings and goings of each 'inmate' are religiously recorded in admission and discharge slips and regularly compiled lists and registers, all for the purpose of ensuring that every eligible shilling of subsidy was secured.

As in the story of Stella Jimbidie of Cherrabun, and one or two other stations, including Louisa Downs, there were some station owners and managers who vigorously opposed the children of the station going to school. Some wanted them as workers. Others believed that education would 'spoil' them. But most of the stations were supportive, and many children headed into Fitzroy on the Mission truck. By the end of the 1950s there were also schools established, with the support of the station owners, on Go Go and Christmas Creek. It was still patchy, but seventy years after the whitefellas arrived in the Fitzroy Valley, significant numbers of children were starting to receive at least a rudimentary education.

Which is not to say they enjoyed the experience, as June Davis recalls:

> *I was only five when I was sent* [to the Mission school] *and finished when I was eighteen years of age. You go in there first we just cried and cried and cried. Even in school you know and teachers bin try to get us to do something good, but we didn't like it. All the big big kids looking after us and, they bin always look after us in school, but big kids always tell us to run away from school.*
>
> *And when I growing up like nine or ten years of age we bin feel like running away. We bin always run away. But we didn't get far. The missionaries would come, pick us up, take us back. Belt um us with a strap. Little short strap. We getting teenagers now. Thirteen years of age.* [We'd say,] *'You wait. We'll go back home and tell our parents on you.'*

Nowhere in the files sighted is there a rationale given for the closure of Moola Bulla, or a suggestion of regret or sorrow over the fate of its residents. But events arising did cause concern among the authorities.

One of the leaders of the 1946 Pilbara strikers had been a white man named Don McLeod. He was seen by the authorities as the evil mastermind

Opposite page: The UAM admission form for Maureen Carter, removed from Moola Bulla with her family at the age of six months. Maureen is now the Chief Executive Officer of the Nindilingarri Cultural Health Service in Fitzroy Crossing.

DEPARTMENT OF NATIVE AFFAIRS.

(To be submitted by Mission in single copy to respective Native Affairs Field Officer)

The United Aborigines Mission
Fitzroy Crossing
W.A.
...........................Mission

....23-7-55......Date

District Officer of Native Affairs,

.........DERBY...........

Dear Sir,

Notification of Admission of Ward (Regulation 55) of an adult native when Departmental subsidy is required by the Mission.

Your approval is requested for the admission of the undermentioned native:

Name ..MAUREEN CARTER..........

Sex FEMALE..... Caste HALF CASTE........

Date of birth 4-1-55

Religion U.A.M.

Father's name GEORGE CARTER..........

Mother's name IVY CARTER

From where received MOOLA BULLA STATION.........

At whose request ....

Date of admission 5TH JULY, 1955.

Reason for admission EX MOOLA BULLA STATION......

....

....

State whether:

(1) Mission to support inmate without Departmental subsidy.
(2) Parents in case of child have arranged to pay maintenance.
(3) Departmental subsidy is requested.

Refer to Circular Memo. No. 290

Court committal case.)
"Agreement" case.) Delete those not
Temporary relief required.) applicable.
Special allowance case.)

Yours faithfully,

B. R. Smoker
w/ Superintendent of Mission

COMMISSIONER OF NATIVE AFFAIRS,

P E R T H.

Recommendation ... Admit to Section 1 subsidy

as from 5.7.55.

AR

Date ....27.7.55 4 AUG 1955 [signature] District Officer.

of those events. McLeod and the strikers maintained their independence, and waged an unceasing battle with the authorities.

McLeod became aware of the impending sale of Moola Bulla. His account of the events that followed is given in his book *How the West Was Lost.*[5] He was seeking to enter into an arrangement with the new owner, a Queensland grazier named Goldman, that would see the Moola Bulla people return to the station, and perhaps eventually buy him out. He and Goldman fell out before they could reach a deal; though it must be said, it seems unlikely that DNW and the government would have allowed any such deal to ever proceed. The Department had no idea exactly what was going on, but the files reveal their paranoia about McLeod.

There is flurry of file notes along the lines of 'receiving disquieting news regarding D. McLeod's movements', a variety of rumours, reports and suspicions noted, one entry saying he is at Moola Bulla with the new owner. The district officer from Derby heads out on patrol to Halls Creek for the specific purpose of checking all this out, but returns with nothing solid. A month later, in October 1955, he heads south to Wallal Station between Broome and Port Hedland, following reports of McLeod 'accompanied by native Jackson' visiting stations between Broome and Wallal.[6]

Their fears of the Pilbara militancy spreading to the Kimberley turned out to be unfounded. It would be 1978 before McLeod and the Strelley Mob, as they were then known,* would establish a presence in the Kimberley through an association with the Yungngora community at Noonkanbah, where they helped the community to establish an independent school.

In the 1950s some of the head stockmen and drovers and leading hands

* Named after Strelley Station near Port Hedland which they had bought and had become their headquarters.

began to apply for citizenship. Sandy Cox, a yard builder on Go Go Station, was one of them.

> *There is a lot of coloured bloke that got his citizens rights you know. They all wanted to drink. That's why they got their citizenship. Eric, Barney, and Darcy,* them three. Archie Doherty, Windy Sharpe, Frank Hunter.*
>
> *I had to get my citizenship, because I wasn't staying at the reserve.** I had to go to the whitefella quarters, stop with the rest of the men. Old Vic Jones, he used to be a good fella and hard too same time, you know, he was a hard man and good fella. He made me have tucker at the table with them.*
>
> *I start put in for citizenship you see. I fill out a paper and I had Eric Lawford helping me too, and we sent that paper away, and I went to the hospital to get examined see, because it was the doctor first to get that paper. I went doctor there, at the old hospital.*
>
> *At the court house the magistrate asked me a few question, why I wanted to drink and all that? You know. And I told him well, I'm a bit shamed trying to go back to camp again, you know, while I'm living there with all the rest of the men see at the quarters, and having tucker with them at the kitchen same time.*
>
> *And you know, I wanted to drink too, that's why. I didn't want to drink with Eric, you know giving me sneaking, otherwise I get*

---

* Three brothers; Eric, Barney and Darcy Lawford.

** Three brothers; Eric, Barney and Darcy Lawford.

Eric in trouble, you know.

And so I got my citizenship rights. [The magistrate] *had to read im out and all that sort of thing, give me all the detail.*

I had to carry them there see in my pocket all the time, I couldn't go without it if I go drinking see, otherwise barmaid, or barman, ask me, 'You got citizenship right?' or I just show em, you know.

Well we used to be right then, go into bar every time we wanted a drink on weekends. Well I know, I was the one, worse one that used to get into trouble all the time too, you know, policeman used to get me. Well I was a bit mad, drinking too much grog. Looking for fight. I'm fighting all the whites there at the bar.

I don't know what they thinking, whites, but you know. Well they served you right but you know some of the bloke didn't like blackfeller drinking there you know, with white men, they keep looking at blokes saying, 'Who's this bloke here?' and saying all that.

Racist, call them, mob of racist. It was good and bad too. Well it was right for me, you know, to go to white man's side and have a drink because I was living at the quarters, you know, with the whites, you know, and so old Vic Jones got used to me in there, you know, I used to drink good there at the station, they used to give us two big bottles [of beer] *every teatime, you know, and go back to bed, every teatime used to have two big bottle.*

Sandy Cox

> *Old Vic Jones, he treat* [me] *as his own bloody right-hand man there you know. I was a good worker. He got me to drive him into town once, we crossed over that river, flood time too. We crossed over there and go round the pub, and he start shouting me.*

As Sandy points out, all of these men who got their citizenship papers were 'coloured', that is, of mixed parentage. It is also clear that their claim to citizenship was all about gaining the right to drink, not about a broader demand for political or social equality. Nevertheless, those who were granted the 'privilege' of citizenship were supposed to live as white men, as Sandy did for a period, living in the white workers' quarters at Go Go. But grog trading across the colour and citizenship lines was rife. Sandy tells stories of his white yard-building colleague at Go Go supplying him and others in the days before he was a citizen:

> *We had this big case, about twenty-four bottles, big ones. Me and old Fred Spinks, we used to get about four cartons of those for Christmas, out on the fence, we done that at Christmas Creek, beside that Bloodwood* [Bore], *you know, we were doing that fence. We had a good drink here at Number Twelve* [Bore], *you know, Number Twelve this side.*

And of he and his fellow citizens supplying their unlicensed friends:

> *They had their eye on me, you know, I was doing it sneaky way, yeah. They never come near see, round the hotel much, you know, I used to give them drink down the bush, sometime, down the river.*

Equal status at law as a citizen did not mean equal wages though.

> *I was only getting four quid a week. Small wages. I don't know* [what the whitefellas were] *getting. More than me anyway, that's for sure you know.*

And eventually Sandy threw in life in the whitefella quarters:

> *Well I pulled out see. Old Vic Jones, he's a rough fella that fella, old man. He was getting a bit too rough, you know. I went down and I stayed down the* [Aboriginal] *camp there, you know. Don Laidlaw grabbed me, and we shift to that station there, Leopold.*

CHAPTER NINE TRAVELLING MEN

That bloke came with a motor car and we put our swag on and then we bin jump on the motor car, went to station, and keep going, old road, you know, going through Christmas Creek, right round. Old road going to old bridge, Fitzroy, we went right round the pub. The old people had a camp you know, by the pub there. We had a camp there one night with old people there.

I sit down there and camped there a couple of days and then we can go from there to Yeeda Station. He had to call Derby to get the car check up you know. Service the motor car, we had to stop there, wait there for nearly one week.

We went from there next through the old Langi crossing. Old road. We didn't go to Broome. We go past. Had to stop in Sandfire, fuel up and keep going to Port Hedland. We had to stop Port Hedland one week and that day we walking round the racecourse, walking round, somebody bin there, might be probably betting horse. We had no money too. After that we fella bin go then. We didn't call in Marble Bar, we just go right through stop in Nullagine and from there bin go, stop in Ethel Creek, and then we went to Balfour Downs. And that's the way we bin see all the mob there. Big mob in there. Working there.

Mervyn Street

In the post-war years more men were moving around the north as drovers, experiencing other parts of the country, and at times receiving decent money at the end of a trip. Tommy May spent many of his younger years droving:

I went to Halls Creek. I got a job in a place called Osmond Valley, that station, other side Halls Creek there [working] for Jack Green. I got stock work there, and droving. Four times, yeah four times, drove into Wyndham meatworks through there.

From there, some kartiya from Vestey's,[*] *they come looking for drovers. They short of drovers, man, anybody. They looking for four blokes. I was one of them, and one boy, Tommy Dart. He is a Queenslander bloke. He's a blackfeller. And Tommy Button, big long fella. And one more boy from somewhere around Coolibah Station.*

Working for a Vestey's drover took Tommy across the border into the Northern Territory:

We been droving with that whitefella bloke, we taking the horses for him, through Daguragu, Wave Hill Station, down past Montejinni

* Vestey's was a British conglomerate with large pastoral holdings in the Northern Territory. Many of their cattle were sold through Wyndham.

Tommy May

there, to that Top Spring, and through that Murranji country. Dry country, scrub country. We went to Newcastle Waters, and Elliot.

Keep going. We went right through to, what's this place, Tennant Creek. Looking for some horses for this Moola Bulla Station. I think that kartiya was looking for them horses to buy them, and put them in a truck, bring them to Moola Bulla Station there. That one kartiya called Steve, Steve Daly they call him ...

We couldn't find horses there and that kartiya bloke left his cattle in a place called Helen Spring, just behind Elliot there, all bin get weak, some of them dying too much.

We take all the horses to a place called Eva Downs. We start work there helping those mob. I got to work there for a couple of months. Mustering and shifting cattle to other waterhole from billabong to windmill ... I worked for two months there.

That's the country — no trees. No wood. No trees. No windbreak.

That bloke, drover bloke, buy us ticket on the bus, you know, going to Darwin, right through. To Darwin right in there. And next two days time we get a plane from there to Wyndham, come home. Back to Halls Creek and Fitzroy. I leave my mate there, somewhere in Wyndham. Tommy Button. He's a Halls Creek boy. And after that I went to Cherrabun.

Mervyn Street travelled more than most. He had been working on Louisa Downs. The new owner, Karl Stein, also owned Balfour Downs in the

Pilbara, among other stations. Stein seems to have been a rough and ready fellow, and a shrewd operator, who had a running feud with DNW over schooling of the Louisa children. He was an illiterate bushie who regarded education as a waste of time, especially for Aboriginal children. DNW files describe him as being of 'poor reputation'.

> *Karl Stein came and brought the station. That's a long story about Karl Stein. He brought a lot of stations. He was good bloke. He really liked old people and kids. When he even go anywhere on the stockcamp, anywhere he bin take load of kids in his motor car you know. He was really good, like a blackfeller Aborigine people. He really liked them. Oh they bin say, 'muluga' or old man.*
>
> *Old Ringer and old Alec and all that other mob, they all went to Balfour Downs but after that, that old man had a truck, a big road train*[*], *he had to go there and when they come back they had to come back in the big truck.*
>
> *Me and Sam Peterson, and another couple of old people from Louisa we were working at old Kupartiya*[**] *there fencing. He picked me and Sam from there and that's the time I bin leave from there now went to Balfour Downs and work ...*
>
> *First job we bin do—we bin go, we had to go out bush, Karl Stein had big truck, two truck, go out Rabbit-proof Fence,*[***] *pulling out all the wire, you know. And first job was that, loading up the truck*

---

* The old Bohemia Downs Station which was, at the time, an outstation of Louisa Downs.

** The old Bohemia Downs Station which was, at the time, an outstation of Louisa Downs.

*** The old Bohemia Downs Station which was, at the time, an outstation of Louisa Downs.

with all the wire, all the netting wire. After that we come back from there, start trapping. Trapping, trapping all the wild cattle. Had to go to bore, to all the places, setting up trap. In the morning go back, see all the cattle in the trap, inside, put them in a truck. Take them back to yard and they bin very wild, you know, very, you know hard to handle with a horse. We had to get them in the yard, quieten them down with the hay and then after that get old cow, quiet cow, then put them outside, tail them out, and then get all the rest out.

When all this mob came back, me and Sam only two blokes left behind.

We had that bloke, Billy Shepherd, he was on the station. Anyway we worked there and then from there we went down to Nullagine, and this bloke called Billy already bin drinking too in the station, and we get to that place Marble Bar, we got there early, about lunch time, go in the pub drinking, drinking, drinking all day until 10 o'clock close at night.

So the bloke got drunk that night. And not far from Nullagine, in a creek there, we nearly got rolled over there. That car end up in the side. Hanging up. In the morning we had a look at it. 'Eh this, we gotta killed night time,' I bin talking to Sam. 'This bloke bin drunk night time.' 'Yeah.' In the morning he bin come and say to me, 'You fella bin want to have beer?'

Kartiya give us a beer. 'What you reckon? You want a drink?' 'Yeah.' Okay we're drinking, trying to forget about that. We bin thinking

Mervyn Street

about that road, you know, that we might have an accident somewhere along road. And he bin k-e-e-p going drinking all the way.

So we pull up halfway, camp for a while there and we stayed there and then he start driving again and that roo shooter kangaroo shooter come along the road and we missed that bloke just by an inch and he turned around and chased us from behind, pulled up and he told that kartiya in front, 'You want to watch where you driving.' He grab that bloke from neck, you know. We went to Marble Bar and I say to Sam, I bin saying, 'I'm not going, following, we might get hurt somewhere you know.' That's the time now we bin stop there, you know. In Marble Bar.

So we go and see cops, two policemen come. 'This bloke drunk and driving might kill us in the road. We can stop here?' 'Yeah. You can stop here.' And one old man bin walking round and asked that old man and that policeman go over that old fella, he bin talk to that old fellow, 'This two young feller want to stop here.' He said, 'Okay? Yeah. You welcome to come, stay here.' At that time he bin say, 'One Kimberley bloke there.' 'Who?' It was Alec Buck.

We bin right now we got somebody there we know, see. Camp one night and then the next morning went to Welfare looking for job. We got job in Coongan Station, sheep station. Worked there. And at the time we had job there, we could have come back home on that time, but we got caught with the other missionary bloke, old Jack Braeside. 'Come with me, I'll show you country.' Back that way now and keep moving back from there, back to Nullagine and back to Jigalong, camped there, into Meekatharra and we get sick of following the old man you know. We wanted job. We bin like to work with station you know.

So in Meekatharra we apply job. Carnegie Station, past Wiluna. That's where we finished up working there and all round and back there. After that we went separate way, you know, we become used to the people. We know them people now. And that's the time I bin go to Mount Clere after Meekatharra. Holiday. I went to Mount Clere Station. I work there for a long time. Meekatharra, back to Mount Clere then back to Mulgul Station, Woodlands Station, Milgun Station. Sundown was working there. From there we kept moving up to Leonora. I was looking for job there, working around there and Alec's brother, Colin, short fellow, he bin ask this bloke, 'You can put this young fellow work this job on the railway line?' 'Yeah. They're welcome to work'. So we work one year doing the railway line.

I used to walk with a big hammer, sledgehammer, banging all this big rail. Up and down. Worked there one year.

From Leonora. Up to Menzies and up to other place there. This side Coolgardie and back again. Up and down. When we bin come over from Kalgoorlie we had to ride train. Free ride because we was working, we was workers. Go up and down and back. Good money.

When I was right near Leonora, there is a big mine there, not far, I was banging all this rail. I find this big nugget laying in the ground. Pick them up.

Go to show the old boss now what I find. He was getting greedy for that thing. I didn't know. You know. Well just like we find some gold, it's nothing to us, we don't believe in this money now, I bin just show him, and he would take him you know. He bin give me his cash.

After that I finished holiday, and I changed my job. I'm going to Cosmo Newberry because Sundown was working there in Cosmo Newberry. When I went to Cosmo Newberry and finished work there, bin go back and, 'Where Sundown?' 'He gone. He finish working here.'

I worked for a little while there, I worked with old Bruce Stone in truck, he was a truckie for carting load from Cosmo to Warburton. You know carting load. Just helping him, you know, I was offsider for him. Go from Cosmo Newberry to Warburton, cart load and truck cattle in the night and bring cattle in and put him on the train.

After I went from there I had a break and I went Kurrawang because old Bob Nunyea was there, and I spent some holiday with him. I bin go there, after that now I was there a little while and I met Ernest Newberry and Bernard Newberry. They said, 'We want to see your country.' 'We'll go back to Kimberley.'

And from there now we start hitch-hiking back. Hitch-hiked all the way. To Wiluna, after we went to Meekatharra and we get that Jigalong truck to Jigalong, and Welfare came from Port Hedland, keep going to Hedland and from the Outlander we got all the young fellows from Broome and they was drunk and we asked them, 'We want a lift back to Broome.' 'Oh no worries. Plenty of room.' We had to get on, that's the only lift back to Broome. After Broome we got missionaries take us to Derby. Then from Derby other missionaries from Fitzroy, old Smoker and that 'nother bloke from Derby. We had to go halfway mark, you know, and get a lift when other missionary come from Fitzroy and then back home.

I was there for a long time. Probably seven years.

It was indeed a long time. And while Mervyn was travelling the Pilbara and the Goldfields, Stein sold Louisa. The new owner, Les Schubert, wrote to DNW:

We are writing to you in regard to several natives that were removed from Louisa Downs over 12 months ago by a previous owner to Balfour Downs. The relatives of the above natives reside on Louisa and are constantly asking for their return. They are wives, children and husbands. The names are as far as we know Ringer and Sam, Jimmy, Marvin, Sundown, Kathleen Ularia and two children. We believe they have no way of returning. The officer in Halls Creek has made attempts to get them returned without success. Please do not disclose the source of this complaint to the previous owner, Karl Stein, as we have business dealings with him. The purpose of the complaint is solely to keep faith with the families employed here and not due to labour shortage. Trust the matter will be followed up. Thanking you. Yours faithfully, Schubert.[1]

The file then contains a series of memos from DNW offices of reported movements and sightings of Mervyn, Sundown and the others. But Mervyn remained elusive, until he made his own way back.

CHAPTER TEN A LOT OF CHANGES

I think there was a lot of changes happening during the 1960s. I can clearly remember that when I started off as a teenager working for the station our rations were very meagre, you know only with flour, tea and sugar and there was a marked change between, I suppose, the issuing of the rations, you know, in the stations where they started within I think early '60s they would start issuing, they were beginning to give out things like WeetBix, Weeties and milk and sugar and that sort of thing. But previously you just only had flour, tea and sugar.

Olive Knight

Ten years after District Officer Pullen's reports of the 1950 Fitzroy Crossing races, with its relatively upbeat accounts of footraces, women shopping and amicably settled labour issues, one of his successors, Welfare Inspector Baldwin, filed reports from the 1960 races that seemed to indicate a much sourer mood.

On his first day in town, Baldwin:

> *Attended the race meeting that afternoon and was approached by a white stockman in a drunken condition and requested that I declare it 'open season on blackfellas' ... He ranted and raved about natives in his camp stealing his food and wanted to know what would happen if he shot one.*[1]

He describes how, before retiring for the night, 'Everything was quiet, there was no fighting amongst the natives, however the white population was grogging on regardless.'[2]

Early the next day he was woken by a Derby man and told that: 'There was a bit of a show last night' and that '50 natives took to 5 white stockmen over some liquor'.[3]

Baldwin's investigations found that:

> *Two blackfellas ... approached two stockmen with the request that they be given some liquor. They were refused and Freddy Wannada threw his arms around the stockman and they fell to the ground. The other native went to Fred's assistance and the other stockman grappled with him. There were approximately 50 natives in the area at the time. This happened near the hotel. The police intervened but by this time the stockmen in the bar had arrived and there were cries of 'shoot the buggers—shootem all'. A few of the stockmen who were not so drunk quietened the mob and 3 natives and 2 white men were arrested on drunk charges and locked up in the gaol.*[4]

Baldwin visited the prisoners, and tried unsuccessfully to find out who had earlier supplied Freddy and the others with liquor. In a telling comment on how the people saw the world of the white station hands, Baldwin writes:

'I asked Freddy Wannada why he had done such a foolish thing and his reply was to the effect that he was a man and that's what men do.'[5]

With people like Tommy May and Mervyn Street travelling widely and experiencing a world beyond the Kimberley, and many of the head stockmen and leading hands acquiring citizenship and buying into the stockmen's drinking culture, the old model of the stations and missionaries having complete power over people's lives was becoming less and less viable. And by the 1960s there were signs here and there of people not just wanting something more, but being prepared to seek it.

The same 1960 report from Welfare Inspector Baldwin of Derby records that at the Mission he was:

> *approached by Alec Rogers and given five pounds to place in his account in Derby. (Alec Rogers is a native who approached me last visit and wanted to buy a block of land build a house and get his children out of the mission to come and live with him. So far I have started off his bank account and this deposit will bring the balance to ten pounds.)*[6]

A 1965 file is a schedule of payments made to pensioners at the Mission. Nearly all of the listed payments show one-third of the total amount as 'cash payment due to pensioner', with the other two-thirds being 'amount payable to organisation', that is, to the UAM. But although there are no details provided, one of the pensioners, Cissie Juboy, must have made representations to the Department of Social Services. She receives the whole of her payment without deduction. There is an annotation: 'As pensioner understands money she is entitled to handle her own affairs. Please make your arrangements re maintenance with her.'[7]

COMMONWEALTH OF AUSTRALIA—DEPARTMENT OF SOCIAL SERVICES

SCHEDULE OF PAYMENTS TO ABORIGINES

DUPLICATE

FORM S.A. 62

AGE, INVALID OR WIDOWS PENSIONS

NAME AND ADDRESS OF ORGANISATION OR WARRANTEE: United Aborigines Mission, Fitzroy Crossing   1011   14/4/66.

PENSION NUMBER	NAME OF PENSIONER	CASH PAYMENT DUE TO PENSIONER	AMOUNT PAYABLE TO ORGANIZATION, ETC.	TOTAL AMOUNT OF PENSION
* 101734	JUBUY Cissie	$180.00		$180.00
¤ 100730	POMILLEE Pompey	8.00	$88.00	96.00
		$188.00	$88.00	$276.00

* Being grant of wife's allowance from 11/11/65 to 14/4/66. As pensioner understands money she is entitled to handle her own affairs. Please make your arrangements re maintenance with her.

¤ Being instalment 14/4/66 at $8.00 pocket money, $22.00 maintenance plus arrears of $6.00 per fortnight payable for children from 11/11/65 to 31/3/66, $66.00, total maintenance = $88.00.
If maintenance for children is not owing over the full period, please credit pensioner's personal account with the amount not payable to the Mission.

United Aboriginies Mission schedule of pensioner payments

Olive Knight remembers a changed mood starting to emerge in the 1960s, when she was a young woman on Go Go Station:

> *I wasn't getting much wages at all. I was just sort of, previous to that, in the early '60s all I got was just rations and clothes you know and then it started to change and then the manager would pay us about $4 a month for our work. So that was a big marked change I thought you know—the wages.*
>
> *The people, the stockmen and the other people, the leaders within our tribes, were beginning to see that they were no longer just pawns in the game of the station owners. They could easily just walk off if they weren't treated right* [over] *money and rations* [or] *if they even heard little rumours about changes of another manager being put there.*
>
> *I can clearly remember one month, one afternoon in the early '60s, these group of men were just walking off the station because they'd heard that this Mr Dawes was going to replace the other manager, Vic Jones, with someone else. There was going to be a takeover but these people were so used to this manager, and didn't want him to leave, and they really showed their, you know, they stood up to Mr Dawes the owner of all of these properties,* * *the Emanuel properties, and said to him, 'Look you're not going to change this. Change the manager. We now are going pack up, get all our swags and we're leaving'. So they all packed up. Everyone. All of us. We went over to Fossil Downs for a little while there.*

---

* The old Bohemia Downs Station which was, at the time, an outstation of Louisa Downs.

Well the management really wasn't aware of us arriving there because we [went] *to a dancing place down on the river. That's where we stayed. We didn't stay there too long.* [...] *Maybe a couple of weeks or so. People start streaming back one by one, two by two and all that. Yeah.*

As Olive says, this walk off did not last long, but nor was it the only such incident. Tim Emanuel, grandson of the Emanuel group's founder, has spoken of frequent 'bust ups'.[8] Olive recalls one such incident:

One of the stories I heard, well just practically a rumour when you come to think of it now it sort of sounds very humorous now, because this leader of a man, a big solid man, I called him uncle, and he stood up and got all these people together and, 'Come here everyone, I want to tell you something, there's something happening at the station and I think someone has heard'—this is his exact words—'that all of the Go Go people are under the gun barrel point.' That's what he said.

'They're on the gun barrel point.' That's what he said. Yeah. And I was thinking what that meant. It didn't register at the time. What was this gun barrel point he was talking about. Later on when he explained it this old man he said, 'Yeah, they're going to shoot the whole of us here.' He was quite a leader. Very very kind of charismatic.

A lot of questioning started and a lot of power recognition I suppose that we were no longer going to be pushed down or told what to do and all that sort of thing. It was building up then.

Between 1963 and 1965 the DNW completed a standardised survey of Western Australian pastoral leases, reporting on the numbers of Aboriginal people, their occupations and wages, education services and attendance, and a subjective assessment of housing conditions.[9] The following tables summarise some of this information for the stations of the Fitzroy Valley.

POPULATION

Station	Rural Workers	Domestic Workers	Pensioners	Children	Other	Total
Calwynyardah	3	4	6	5		18
Cherrabun	26	28	9	41	4	108
Crossing Inn	3	5	2	5	2	17
Ellendale	3		2	2	1	8
Fossil Downs	17	13	10	17	4	61
Go Go	46	34	15	73		168
Jubilee	12	11	3	7	4	37
Kalyeeda	4	6	3	1		14
Leopold Downs	9	6	2	11	1	29
Louisa Downs	22	18	3	17		60
Millijidee	4	2			3	9
Noonkanbah			8			8
Quanbun	3	6	4	6		19
TOTAL	152	133	67	185	19	556

The reports are taken from DNW patrols dating between 1963 and 1965, and as such, there could be some overlap and some gaps. There are also anomalies, such as the figure of only eight pensioners living at Noonkanbah; a 1966 patrol report lists fifty-nine people, including thirty-nine working adults.[10]

Nor is this data comprehensive. The UAM Mission is not included. Nor are Bohemia Downs, Brooking Springs, Christmas Creek and Louisa Downs stations.

Comparable figures for Louisa Downs have been included in the tables based on a 1964 patrol report with comprehensive data.[11] A 1964 patrol report lists nineteen people living at Bohemia Downs.[12] The nearest data for Brooking Springs is a 1959 patrol report listing seventy-five people resident on the station.[13] No files are available for Christmas Creek after 1950, but there was always a large community of around 100 people living there. A 1965 Register of Inmates for the UAN Mission lists 145 people.[14]

If these figures for Bohemia, Brooking Springs, Christmas Creek and the UAM, totalling around 339 people, are added into the survey figure of 556, it gives an Indigenous population in the Fitzroy Valley in the mid 1960s of approximately 895 people, or in round terms, 900.

EDUCATION

Station	Children of School Age	Number at School
Calwynyardah	0	0
Cherrabun	11	0
Crossing Inn	4	4
Ellendale	1	1

Fossil Downs	12	12
Go Go	47	47
Jubilee	1	1
Kalyeeda	0	0
Leopold Downs	4	4
Louisa Downs	10	0
Millijidee	0	0
Noonkanbah	0	0
Quanbun	0	0
UAM Mission	45	45
TOTAL	135	114

In this table the figures for the UAM have been derived from adding up those in the June 1965 Register for whom the Mission is claiming Living Away From Home Allowance, and it is assumed that all are attending the Mission school.

It can be seen that by the mid 1960s most children in the Fitzroy Valley were receiving some form of education, with schools at the Mission, and Go Go and Christmas Creek stations. There is quite possibly some overlap, with the children listed for Fossil Downs and Leopold Downs attending the Mission school.

The anomalies are Cherrabun and Louisa Downs stations. The Cherrabun survey in 1964 notes that construction of a school there is scheduled to start in 1965. Until then, as Stella Jimbidie said, the station management had been adamantly opposed to the Cherrabun kids being taken away to the Mission school. At Louisa, the idiosyncratic Karl Stein continued to be uncooperative with DNW. There are even suggestions, not substantiated, of 'information tending to suggest that schoolage children were being locked in a shed on the arrival of the Native Welfare Officer at Louisa Downs'.[15]

The following table sets out the numbers employed and rates of pay for those 'Rural Workers', the classification used for men. In 1964, the middle year of the DNW survey, the male basic wage in Western Australia was fifteen pounds and eleven shillings per week.[16]

EMPLOYMENT & WAGES ('RURAL WORKERS')

Wages shown in pounds and shillings per week

Station	Number Employed	Common Wage	Highest Wage	Lowest Wage
Calwynyardah	3	1–10	2–10	1–0
Cherrabun	26	1–0	1–0	0–5
Crossing Inn	3	2–0	3–0	1–0
Ellendale	3	4–0	5–0	4–0
Fossil Downs	17	1–0	1–10	1–0
Go Go	46	2–10	12–0	0–12
Jubilee	12	3–0	3–0	3–0
Kalyeeda	4	1–5	1–5	1–0
Leopold Downs	9	4–0	4–0	2–0
Louisa Downs	22	4–0	5–0	2–0
Millijidee	4	3–0	3–15	2–5
Noonkanbah	0			
Quanbun	3	4–0	4–0	4–0

Women were described as 'Domestic Workers'. The female basic wage at the time was eleven pounds thirteen shillings a week:[17]

EMPLOYMENT & WAGES ('DOMESTIC WORKERS')

Wages shown in pounds and shillings per week

Station	Number Employed	Common Wage	Highest Wage	Lowest Wage
Calwynyardah	4	1–5	1–5	1–5
Cherrabun	28	0–10	1–0	0–10
Crossing Inn	5	1–0	3–0	1–0
Ellendale				
Fossil Downs	13	0–15	1–0	0–10
Go Go	34	0–10	2–10	0–10
Jubilee	11	1–10	3–0	1–10
Kalyeeda	6	0–10	0–10	0–10
Leopold Downs	7	0–17	1–0	0–10
Louisa Downs	18	1–0	1–0	1–0
Millijidee	2	1–0	1–0	1–0
Noonkanbah	0			
Quanbun	6	2–0	2–0	2–0

Clearly there had been significant increases since the first introduction of wages in 1950, when the voluntary scheme agreed by the Pastoralists Association had allowed for a rate of one pound per month for men and ten shillings per month for women. These same amounts had become the base weekly rate, indicating a fourfold increase. And many stations were paying above this base rate, with some stations paying substantially more. There is a huge variation; the standard stockman's wage is a pound a week at two of the big, established stations of Cherrabun and Fossil Downs, and four times this at Leopold Downs, and Karl Stein's Louisa Downs.

The Cherrabun survey was undertaken in November of 1963, and the one at Go Go in November 1965. Even so, the discrepancies between these two properties, both owned by the Emanuel group, are startling. On Cherrabun it is a flat pound a week to men and ten shillings a week to women, with only one or two exceptions. At Go Go, most men and women are on two pounds ten shillings a week, but with significant variations and gradations both above and below this common rate.

Interestingly, a detailed report in 1962 says Go Go is paying exactly the same standard wage as at Christmas Creek, the other station in the Emanuel group, and states that this amount is two pounds per month.18 So either wages at Go Go increased fivefold from two pounds a month to two pounds ten shillings a week in the course of three years, or, one must speculate, it increased by twenty-five per cent, and the comprehensive DNW survey got it wrong, and listed the monthly wage as a weekly wage.

These huge discrepancies in percentage terms between individuals doing the same jobs on properties in such a limited geographical area can only happen when the starting base is extremely low.

CHAPTER ELEVEN YOU DON'T TELL ME WHAT TO DO

What emerges from the DNW's stations survey of the early 1960s is a patchwork of station by station arrangements, in some senses not unlike the old days, where conditions, and now wages, are dependent on the attitudes and needs of individual managers and owners.

Conditions remained harsh and very basic on all properties. And on some they remained 'appalling', literally. This is the one-word description of the housing at Noonkanbah in 1965 in the statewide survey.[1]

At stations like Noonkanbah and Louisa Downs people still lived in humpies cobbled together from scrap materials. The Louisa Downs camp is described in a 1966 report:

> *The camp itself is a big health hazard some ½ mile from the station. Water is rolled over from the station in 44 gallon drums ... Sanitation is nil, no toilets of any kind are in existence in or near the camp, the only thing to do is go bush. Washing and laundry facilities are also non-existent at the camp.*[2]

This bureaucratic assessment echoes almost exactly Mervyn Street's recollection of the 'rough life' at Louisa, down to the absence of water, washing and laundry facilities.

In 1962 a DNW officer reported of Leopold Downs:

> *There is a constant traffic of natives to and from this station, which is not surprising in view of the poor conditions. The manager was absent, so that, as yet I have been unable to ascertain if there will ever be a change in conditions. There is a poor employer-employee relationship ... From speaking to other station staff it would appear that the thought of natives washing, or performing natural bodily functions, is a farcical idea on this station.*[3]

Reports of the time also analyse the rations given out at some stations, especially in relation to pensioners, who had no option but to cash their cheques at the station where they lived; there were no post-office boxes at the time, and no means of transport into town. In practice, the station bookkeeper or storekeeper handled all the paperwork, and the individuals would never sight the actual cheque.

In 1966 the old age pension was $24 per fortnight. At Louisa Downs, out of their $12 per week, each pensioner was receiving $1 a week in pocket money, and rations valued by a Social Security inspector at $7.80 per week, indicating that the station was pocketing over $3 per week per pensioner; and as indicated by the description of the camp, they could hardly claim to be covering power, water or any other expenses.[4]

At Noonkanbah, in the same year, the station claimed to be giving pensioners between $1 and $3 per week pocket money (though the inspector found no evidence of anyone receiving $3) and the weekly ration was listed and costed at $3.59, with the pensioners buying additional food at the station store out of their pocket money. The inspector calculated that even allowing for the maximum $3 pocket money, the total value being received was $6.59, meaning the station was making over $5 per pensioner per week.[5]

A 1962 report attempts a similar analysis in relation to workers at Go Go after 'receiving numerous complaints re the low wages and requests that I approach the manager for a rise'.[6] It makes what it describes as generous estimates in relation to the value of clothing, food and accommodation, and adds these to the cash wage, and concludes: 'Thus a single male native, working from sun up to sun down (with a ½ hour break at noon) is paid 6 pounds 10 shillings in cash or "benefits".'[7]

At the same time another memo goes through a similar set of calculations in relation to child endowment and aged and invalid pensions at Christmas Creek and Go Go, and the writer concludes that 'it is my opinion that the use of this money is being considerably abused ... [and] it will be seen that from 1 to 2 pounds per fortnight [of pension payments] is unaccounted for'.[8]

It is a mixed picture. In 1961 there is a case of malnutrition at Go Go. In June of 1962 there are complaints about wages, and the above analysis of abuse and exploitation. Yet in the same file, for the same year, an April 1962 report is very upbeat, stating, 'All the natives appeared very happy and quite content.'[9]

These discrepancies in the Go Go file for 1962 are perhaps the starkest example of a pattern that becomes apparent in reading the DNW station files. The commentary in the reports is clearly dependent on the attitudes of the individual officers, and factors such as their personal relationships with different station managers.

The Emanuel brothers group of stations—Go Go, Christmas Creek and Cherrabun—are particularly interesting. For decades they had the biggest of the Aboriginal camps in the Fitzroy Valley, especially at Go Go and

Christmas Creek, and were the largest employers. They had a reputation of being reasonably fair and enlightened in their attitudes. There is no doubt that they were proactive in allowing and assisting the establishment of schools on each of their properties at a time when this was most uncommon on pastoral properties.

At Go Go and Cherrabun in the 1950s and early '60s they made comparatively generous investments in facilities for the station camps, which were regarded as being as good as any in the district, except perhaps Fossil Downs. This amounted to Nissen huts with bare earth floors, as described by Jimmy and Joy Shandley:

> *Jimmy: Go Go had little shelter. Like, you know, them little Army huts. They used to call them Army things but no concrete floor, no power but they had water tank.*
>
> *Joy: Oh yeah but no running water like in the houses. We had to go to the bathroom ...*
>
> *Jimmy: No separate toilet.*

And even the provision of education was seen to have its limits. In 1962 the principal of the school at Go Go hatched the idea of taking his students to Perth to see the Empire Games. As he explained:

> *The teacher considers that the children have now gone beyond the stage where they require a good basic English vocabulary. They now need experiences and sights to use their vocabulary on ... The management of Go Go refuse to countenance any suggestion of such a trip. The teacher also reports that, in several cases children*

have accompanied their parents tending bores or boundary riding, resulting in anything up to a year's break in education. Boys, on turning fourteen, are becoming stockmen etc even though they may show a fair degree of scholastic ability. The management in these cases is not at all sympathetic or helpful.' [10]

These reports tally closely with the experience of Jimmy Shandley, who attended the Go Go school. He was born in 1953, and the experience he describes would have been a few years later, but the manager of Go Go, Vic Jones, was the same:

Well I didn't actually finish like going away to high school or anything like that. Old Vic Jones, us boys, he just kept sending us to the stock you know. My aim was to become a diesel motor mechanic. That's why I fiddle around with a lot of vehicles. There was no opportunity for us to go.

He said to my dad one day, I still remember, he said, 'You send that boy away he won't get a job back here again.' I still remember that. But anyway I worked out in the stock camp for a little while and then they put me back to the workshop. Go Go where the original workshop is now.

I was only young still and they put me with a mechanic and Vic Jones said, 'That's your offsider.' So he was my boss. He told me, 'Your job is to clean up, keep that workshop tidy.' And so from there I just kept going and going. But I knew, like after a while now, I can remember there is no thing like training or anything to become now what I am.

Jimmy Shandley

Jimmy would go on to become one of the youngest ever head stockmen on Go Go Station, but only at the cost of toeing the line, being denied an opportunity for further education, and of fulfilling his dream of becoming a mechanic.

Jimmy's wife Joy also grew up at Go Go. As she makes clear in this account, her family, the Nuggetts, also felt Vic Jones' wrath. Joy's father was a desert man who came in and settled at Go Go, and worked for the station for many years, the 1960s when he got a job as a gardener at the Go Go school:

> *Most of my people came and worked on the station, where they were placed, even though their land was way out in the Great Sandy Desert. And before, maybe in the '40s, or '30s, or '20s, most of our people migrated into pastoral country, a few of them went to Christmas Creek and then placed onto Go Go because of previous family already been there. And, for example, my grandmother she came through with her brother, his grandfather and their family. My father came later I think in the '50s from the Canning Stock Route area right back to the Great Sandy Desert. Came, worked there and lived there basically. My grandmother passed away, she died on Go Go and this is why we have connection to it. It's not our country. It's Gooniyandi country and we respect the traditional land around that, you know, growing up and working within the group.*
>
> *It was a good relationship in those days, they worked together and they shared the country and there were mutual marriages between our people and their people. And even though they were bushmen, they came and worked on the yards. My dad worked with old*

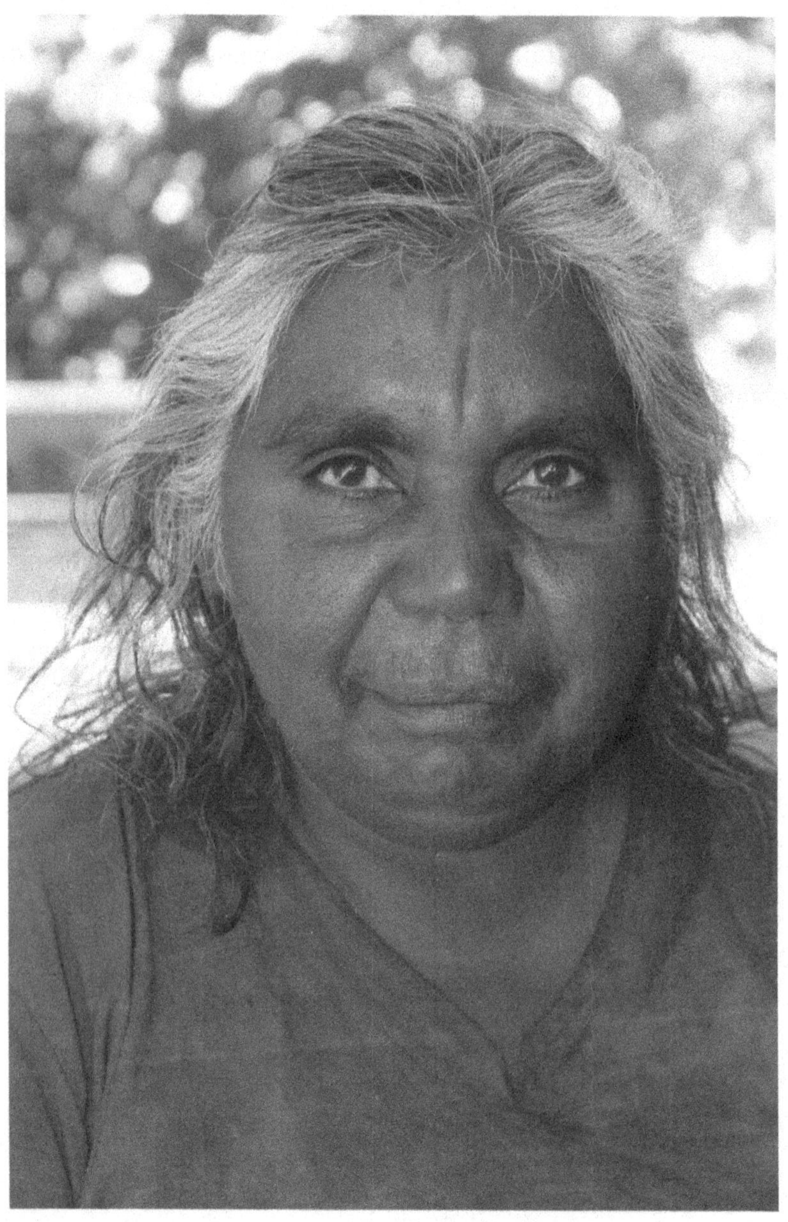

Joy Nuggett

Sandy Cox, and other old man, and they saw most of these people you know, and we grew up with them and respecting them too. But incidents like shooting dogs and things like that, it did happen to us at one stage.

*Vic Jones was there. He was a bit of a hard manager, a hard man. Some of these old people might know him but he was very, he had a bit of animosity towards my dad. I don't know why. I think when they had first government school there, after the cave school** *they were looking for a gardener, and I didn't know this until later, right back in the 80s, one of the principals wrote a letter back to us and explained my dad, his character and stuff like that.*

Because everybody was owned by the station, they were controlling the works and stuff like that, they didn't want anybody to break away because they thought that man might be setting bad example for the others. When my dad, when he became the school gardener, when the first school was built, Vic Jones didn't like it, he said.

At one stage we came across on [law] *business to spend time at the old Mission, because my granny and my grandfather lived over there, and Mum and I, like most of us came across, that was during the floods, in December. And by January, February, we was supposed to go back, Dad was supposed to go back, but I think what happened maybe, when the manager asked where he was, how come he didn't turn up for work on Go Go as a station hand, he didn't show up because he asked to be the gardener at*

* The first school at Go Go, established in the late 1950s, was in a large cave in a hill near the station.

the school so he was ready to go to the school to work and then the manager said to him, 'Don't come back because you don't work for us anymore.' So he was hunted out from the station camp, they had a station reserve, you know those little tin houses.

And so we was stuck on this side, because we were told stories that Dad moved from the Mission, they used to stay around Billy Goat Reserve, you know where the footbridge is, waiting for the river to go down. And after the flood went down, the principal came across and he said, 'Where's my gardener?'I want you coming back to start work,' and Dad said, 'No we can't go back because the manager said, "You can't come back to the station".'

My dad said to the principal, Mr Cane, 'If you want me back you have to find a place for me and my family to live.' So he might have negotiated with the station or maybe with the Emanuel company or maybe with the government ...

He agreed with the government, the principal, to acquire a bit of an excision behind the school. And that's the time he got his own corner there, because he worked with the school.

That's how we moved behind the school but we had a good life because dad was on a proper wage, you know, he wasn't on that Centrelink payments or whatever they used to call them, social security. He was on a proper wage and we lived a good life. We had food, we had stores. My dad was, I don't know for a bushman because he worked as a gardener, he survived you know, self-sufficient. He had his own garden and had to, because the station

> *couldn't give us meat. I don't know why, because they never got on well, because since he moved away and worked for the school.*
>
> *And that's where we saw the change. He* [Jones] *can't let us live in the station but then he started sending workers, kartiya workers to tie knots on the hoses and even at movie nights we might've been at the movies in the school, he'd go behind my parents' camp and shoot the dogs. We used to come back and all our dogs were wounded.*
>
> *But then at one stage, he just stood up, he couldn't hack that any more, my dad approached him at the station. Annette, you remember that story where Dad bin go and him and old Vic Jones had argument and he said to him, 'I don't work for you. I work for the government. You don't tell me what to do.' For an Aboriginal person to stand up ...*

Annette Kogolo was sitting with her sister, Joy, and Jimmy as this story was being told, and she took up the account:

> *I think Dad was the first person, we had that little piece of land there. We had our own little private camp that he looked after. He put a fence around it, built bough sheds, and we lived in a tent and went to school. Nothing to do with station where everybody else lived.*

Joy summed up:

> *At that time we felt that we've got a place of our own, which is good, but only because of that bad situation that he went through with*

Annette Kogolo

the pastoralist. The government, the principal at that time didn't want him to go away because he wanted him to be employed by the school.

I mean [Dad] *worked for the station before just for ration and clothing and whatever, boot and hat and stuff, alongside Sandy building fences and troughs and yards and stuff, even he used to work as a bore mechanic, not bore mechanic, but helping the bore person put holes in the ground.*

Basically as soon as he didn't work for station, the manager didn't want him in the camp.

For all the changes that had taken place, in the mid 1960s a Kimberley station owner or manager still regarded his station as an empire where his word was law. But no longer was this being accepted as unquestioningly as it once had been.

CHAPTER TWELVE AN UNWRITTEN LAW NO MORE

On 27 January 1969, in the middle of the wet season, with the river rising, an event occurred that would change the face of Fitzroy Crossing forever.

Joe Brown, who would go on to become the chairman of the Kimberley Aboriginal Law and Cultural Centre, among other leadership positions, was a young stockman on Go Go Station at the time. As Joe tells his story:

> *Round about Christmas time all them stations used to have holiday. This one Christmas time all the Wangkatjungka mob bin come all the way down from Wangkatjungka*[*] *and they walked halfway to between Price Bore* [and] *Forrest Bore ... and then right up to Go Go. So we was there. ... I might have been 17 or 18 that all I was, you know, youngfella. We bin having a big corroboree there every night from all day you know ...*
>
> *And that was '68, and then I think old Scrivener* [the Go Go Manager] *didn't like people bin singing all the time very loud you*

* From Christmas Creek Station.

know ... And then next morning two tractor come along and he had young fellow manager that Kevin Norton round everybody up. 'Come on you mob got to jump on this tractor ... Come on you mob. We don't want you mob staying here. You only making a lot of humbug.'

He just bin get all the Christmas Creek mob, whole lot of them. This mob expecting they gotta go back to Christmas Creek, you know them old fellas jumping on the tractor and [Norton said], *'We going to take you mob and leave you mob in the Fitzroy.' They thought they want to go back to Christmas Creek but this bloke taking other action. He took them right down to where that crossing,* other side of crossing, get them there and two tractor come back with nothing ...*

He just telling them, 'Well you mob bin staying right here.' You know. Didn't say anything about who's going to pick them. He just bin left them there. He said, 'You not allowed to go back to Go Go.'

I think that Christmas Creek manager didn't like them you know ... That's why he ring this bloke in Go Go ... And the Go Go bloke just picked them people and take them into and left them in Fitzroy ...

[The Christmas Creek manager] *rang him up, maybe he might even say to them, 'Get rid of them mob. Don't bring them back here, take them down to Fitzroy.' Well that Mission fix them, you know, or the government or policeman.*

---

* The old low level Fitzroy River crossing.

Joe Brown

I was living on Go Go that time. Anyway next morning well we had our family in that mob too, me and other brother of mine we bin walk with other two old fellow. We walk all the way from station, from Go Go, from the community where we living, we bin get there.

All right we walk down, get other side of river where we can see all this mob. They was really all hungry. No feed. They want to get across the river. Anyway the other brother of mine old Jimmy Bieunderry come along with a big red truck from Mission, pull up other side and then he drive into police station and ask policeman if we can get a boat to cross this old people? He say, 'No let them mob find their way.'

Policeman told him like that, 'You can cross them. Get them 'cross.' And then so, but like by this time we were start crossing those old people. We had a lot of good old strong people you know, all them mob. Tommy May was there too. He was in a mission before. He [help] *them cross them across the river. Long that bridge, we had all of them.*

Some old people were very frightened you know, we had take them very nice and safety get across. We had two old people we carry you know. Strong old people.

That water was just rising up. About that much. Around about the leg. And they bin frighten because they're the desert people. Old people from that side too you know. They don't know much about river. Anyway we had to cross them.

Well he bin take all day because biggest mob. Well we put 'em in a raft. We wrapped 'em up all the swag and put a calico [canvas], *you know, big tent. You bin tie them up and when you tie it up he just float. You can just push them along very nice and easy, he float like boat you know and we had to put few old people 'cross and push them. Make them like they don't look.*

*Yeah. We had to push them across and get all everybody that side and then big truck was load them ... So we bin looked this place,** *find a place for the people. Old Jimmy and other old people like they found out this a good place for these people you know because this creek always go up you know.*

We had to drive them just, right down here. We camped with them you know. Just spinifex ... Clear the ground. All this area where the roadhouse and Kurnangki [Community] *now just bin spinifex. We had to trap them, then the old people had to clean all the spinifex and make a tent; this where the* [Brooking Channel] *bridge is now we had that steep place where we were going to get down to that river. I mean to that water. That's where the old people were staying ...*

People been used to living in humpy you know. We didn't worry about life, long as they had calico, you know tent. We set 'em up and that's why, you know, give you a try where you want to sleep right in town. They had a tent all along there.

---

* This interview with Joe Brown was conducted at the offices of KALACC, at the front of Kurnangki Community, only a couple of hundred yards from where the Christmas Creek refugees set up their camp on the west bank of the Brooking Channel.

> *Old Jimmy Bieunderry and Mission had to help them and they was doing all the ringing up to the government and then they start social for the people ... Social Security mob and from there they had to feed them, like all the tucker and water in a drum and tractor. Old people used to drive a tractor down there. Old fellow old Barnaby used to drive. For bringing ngapa,** *you know, with that tractor.*

At this time Olive Knight was married to Jimmy Bieunderry, who has since passed away. He had been one of the last of the Walmajarri people to come in from the desert. As a young adult he had gone to the Mission school in Fitzroy Crossing, determined to become literate. Olive and Jimmy lived at the UAM and worked as missionaries, as Olive tells:

> *Jimmy was a part missionary. And the Welfare came and suddenly just offered some positions to the leading men you know and he was one of them because they saw his potential in leadership you know.*
>
> *It was a shock to see these people suddenly out on the banks of Fitzroy Crossing. This side of the bank anyway, wanting to get in to Fitzroy.***
>
> *What I can remember of it is that it was almost the end of the wet season I think, and they brought them in, and they all sort of left at the old bridge there and people were calling out for help*

---

* 'Ngapa' is the Walmajarri word for water.

** This interview with Olive Knight was conducted at the Wangkatjungka Community, on the south side of the Fitzroy River, the same side the people were stranded.

from there and they were starving, you know, they didn't have food or anything so the water over the low bridge was I think above the knee.

And so Jim went down with a group of men and had to help these people cross, you know. There were no boats or anything. He went down and went to, I think got the Mission to help him and all that and load, you know, sort of guided the people across the flooded section. Some of them were old and all that so he sort of made that many trips you know guiding all these people across the flooded bridge and got them safely to the other side.

They were scared and they were lost because they had just left the place where they belonged, where they had lived all their life just about. Old people. And so, I think they were scared because they were going into a different tribal country you know, traditionally, because previously every tribal people feared each other you know and there'd be tribal killings and all this sort of thing. But anyway when they came, they were so brave these people, they came in thinking the worst but at the same time want to sort of find some sort of life in a new place you know.

Brooking Channel, that's where he sort of set up camp for them. Got wood and everything. He worked hard that day I clearly remember and when he finally got them all settled there it was dark and they had to find the wood you know and start up fires for them and the Mission sort of gave them a lot of food and settled them down there in tents.

Jimmy Bieunderry

Olive Knight

The events caused alarm among the authorities. The first entries are torn from a notepad and placed in a file that was subsequently created.[1] They are handwritten notes from Kevin Johnson, the Acting Superintendent in the Derby office of DNW. On 28 January he writes:

> *—Xmas Creek—*
>
> *9.30am Bruce Smoker UAM FX rang to advise 150 natives ex Xmas Creek camped over the river. Smoker visited them and they have no food and very little money. Women and children only have bank books with average approx $3 credit.*
>
> *No money apparent in camp. Natives left Xmas Creek walkabout to Go Go for ceremony etc and subsequently carted to the river from Go Go in 3 tractor/trailer loads.*
>
> *From Mr Smoker's questioning people not returning to Xmas Creek and are still some more to come. Smoker also has some Xmas Creek natives in mission.*
>
> *Police will assist and ferry natives across river into FX—can camp at emergency site.*[2]

But by later the same day, it seemed the police had changed their minds about providing assistance. It suggests Joe Brown's comments about the police refusing to help Bieunderry are right on the mark. Perhaps they had rung the Go Go manager. Johnson's note continues:

> *Rang Tom Carlson* [a police constable in Fitzroy Crossing].

> *Go Go natives get ration every Sunday from Station—Xmas and Cherrabun can obtain from their own Stations only. Tom says no urgent panic, plenty bush tucker and guns in camp.*[3]

Three days later, with the Christmas Creek mob now established in a camp by the Brooking Channel, Carlson has clearly spoken to the Christmas Creek manager, and he and the DNW are worried. Johnson's file note of 31 January says:

> *Rang Const Carlson FX*
>
> *Tom now advises that 3 trailer loads of Xmas Creek natives (approx 100) brought to FX are bushed.*
>
> *If they find their way back to Xmas Creek, management will enlist police to have natives removed from the property.*
>
> *Const Carlson requests and strongly urges that* [DNW officers] *visit FX very near future and investigate and discuss at first-hand.*[4]

His file note then has three queries, suggesting that the strategy is to return the mob to Christmas Creek if at all possible:

> 1. *Can natives be removed from the pastoral lease property legally?*[5]

A subsequent margin note with double underlining simply says, 'No.'

> 2. *Can portion of tribal lands be reserved for natives habitation?*[6]

31.1.69

Rang Const Carlson F.X. A.

Tom now advises that 3 trailer loads of Xmas Creek natives (approx 100) bought to F.X. are bushed.

If they find their way back to Xmas Creek, management will enlist police to have natives removed from the property.

Const Carlson requests + strongly urges that Supt + A/S visit FX very near future + investigate + discuss at first hand.

Query: (i) Can natives be removed from the pastoral lease property legally? – No

Yes (ii) Can portion of Tribal lands be reserved for Natives habitation?

(iii) Const. Carlson wants a direction as to whether he can legally remove these natives from Xmas Creek if requested by Emmanuel Bros to do so.

[signature]
A/S

Acting Superintendent, Kevin Johnson's file note, Department of Native Affairs, Derby office

The margin note, also double underlined, says, 'Yes.'

> 3. *Const Carlson wants a direction as to whether he can legally remove these natives from Xmas Creek if requested by Emmanuel* [sic] *Bros to do so.*[7]

There is no margin note against this third item. Telegrams to and from DNW head office seek advice on the matter, without getting a clear answer. On 4 February, Johnson sends a telegram via the Flying Doctor radio service used by the stations, addressed to The Manager, Christmas Creek: 'Please advise if Christmas Creek natives now in Fitzroy Crossing have been permanently discharged.' The next day he receives a reply: 'Re tel yes—Manager.'[8]

It has not been possible to establish just what was going on in the minds of the Go Go and Christmas Creek managers, and the young stockman Kevin Norton who drove the tractor backwards and forwards three times from Go Go to the old crossing during that wet season of 1968, but it seems they were angry men. Subsequent events seem to suggest that they were acting at their own initiative rather than with any direction or blessing from the Emanuel brothers' head office in Perth. But in a sense, that briefest of possible replies from the Christmas Creek Station manager brought to an end an unspoken three-way consensus between government, pastoralists and Aboriginal people, and a phase of history that had lasted since the end of the Jandamarra wars.

The Emanuels had held their properties since the 1890s, taking them up soon after the MacDonalds established Fossil Downs. Tim Emanuel, grandson of the pastoral kingdom's founder, had become involved in the management of the group in the 1950s, after an English education and time in Africa. He has described the consensus this way:

> *There was a sort of unwritten law that it was our station but their country. Maybe it was luck or maybe it was good management but it was a very good philosophy which allowed both sides to respect each other's position. I remember frequent occasions when there would be some terrible bust-up and the manager would be abused up and down dale by somebody from the camp. But they would never ever be told to get off the station, they would be told to go back to the camp and that was it. We did consider it always their country. Which was good, it worked.*[9]

It was an unwritten law that was not universally accepted in the Kimberley. But there was a real basis to Emanuel's description—until January 1968, that is, when two of his managers chose to disregard it.

However one describes its underpinnings—unwritten law, consensus, mutual understanding; and whatever one's attitude to the old station system—paternal benevolence, mutually beneficial, or feudal and exploitative—the status quo had been growing more and more fragile. And when the dam burst, a torrent of change was unleashed.

The history and politics and interpretation of the events in the latter half of the 1960s are hotly contested. What is indisputable is that anyone with their eye on the ball could see that change was coming.

CHAPTER THIRTEEN THE STORM CLOUDS BUILD

There were rumours at that time ... that the basic wage was going to come in. That's why people started feeling fidgety you know because they heard rumours that a lot of them were going to be chucked off the station.

Olive Knight

Several years before the pivotal incident with the Christmas Creek mob, in 1965, the Northern Australian Workers Union (NAWU) had launched what became known as the Equal Wages Case in the Commonwealth Conciliation and Arbitration Commission. The case was heard solely in the Northern Territory, and applied specifically to the pastoral industry there.[1] NAWU ran the case entirely on the point of principle of equal pay for equal work, regardless of race. Not a single Aboriginal witness was called. In fact, the involvement of the people who were the subject of the hearing was essentially zero. Barrister Hal Wootten, who represented the pastoralists in the hearings, recalled many years later:

> *There was no contact with Aborigines by anybody in the case, the union advocate, the judges or anybody; the Aborigines were completely outside. They weren't parties to the case, they weren't witnesses. It was all white fellows arguing about them and what ought to happen to them. In today's language it was the greatest denial of self-determination that one could imagine.*[2]

In opposition to the minimalist case of NAWU the Northern Territory pastoralists presented extensive evidence, and in scenes foreshadowing hearings of the Native Title Tribunal in more recent years, took the whole court of commissioners, lawyers and hangers-on out to station country. Essentially they argued two points. First, that many of the Aboriginal employees were 'slow workers' not worthy of equal wages. Second, that if equal pay was implemented there was no way they could pay whole station communities, and there would be disadvantage to them, and enormous disruption to the communities.

There is no question that the case represented an enormous threat to the established economics of the northern pastoral industry. Using the figures from the 1963–65 DNW survey, if the most common wage on each station is used, the average wage of a male Aboriginal station worker in the Kimberley was under £2.50, or $5 after the decimal currency conversion of 1966. NAWU was seeking to convert them to the Commonwealth's pastoral award, which in 1966 was $38.05 for a station hand. In other words, a straight application of the award would mean a rise in the order of 750 per cent for the average worker.

But the tide of time and public sentiment had run out on the pastoralists and left them stranded. In March of 1966 the Commission decided that:

> *The guiding principle must be to apply to Aborigines the standards which the Commission applies to all others unless there are overwhelming reasons why this should not be done. The pastoralists have openly and sincerely explained their problems and future intentions. However they have not discharged the heavy burden of persuading us that we should depart from standards and principles which have been part of the Australian arbitration system since its inception. We do not flinch from the results of this decision which we consider is the only proper one to be made at this point in Australia's history. There must be one industrial law, similarly applied to all Australians, Aboriginal or not.*[3]

While coming down on the side of equal pay, in recognition of the pastoralists' arguments, the Commission allowed a three-year phase-in period before the decision would take effect. The ruling also acknowledged the likely consequences of its decision, and the position taken by the Commonwealth Government:

> *If any problems of native welfare whether of employees or their dependants arise as a result of this decision, the Commonwealth Government has made clear its intention to deal with them. This is not why we have come to our conclusion but it means we know that any welfare problems which arise will be dealt with by those most competent to deal with them.*[4]

Olive Knight recalls the growing unrest of the mid 1960s:

> *Some of* [the rumours about the basic wage] *were just mixed messages and things like that. So they didn't hear it direct from the station. They must have heard it in a roundabout way you know from jackaroos that were working on the station or whoever it was ...*
>
> *I can remember that* [Jimmy] *was aware of some big things, some interruption in the station life, so somehow I think he was sort of somehow expressing some feelings there that there was going to be an influx of visitors into Fitzroy Crossing and that Fitzroy ought to be prepared for this you know and a lot of them were his people from here* [Christmas Creek].

The record shows that Bieunderry did communicate these feelings and fears to the authorities. Two months before the Christmas Creek mob were evicted, he had taken Kevin Johnson of DNW to the site where they finished up, and recommended it to him. A memo headed 'Emergency Camping Site' reads:

> *On 18.11.68 inspected a site (recommended by J. Bieunderry) approx 3 miles west of FX between Highway and Fitzroy River. An excellent block of fertile soil on medium high ground overlooking Fitzroy River ... The site overlooks a pool in the Fitzroy that is an Aboriginal rendezvous and picnic place.*[5]

Well before this, there had been indications of change. The owners of Noonkanbah Station had long held a miserly attitude to their Aboriginal workers and residents. Late in 1966, presumably with the Northern Territory decision in mind, they issued orders to the manager, who wrote to DNW in

Derby: 'I have been instructed by my Directorate to cut down on number of natives on Noonkanbah, as you will realise this is not easy to do.'[6]

His letter was asking DNW to redirect a number of pension and child endowment payments to Nerrima Station, where he had found employment for some of the men. Others were forced to go into the Mission in Fitzroy Crossing.

The UAM was starting to accommodate increasing numbers of individuals and families from the surrounding stations, like those evicted from Noonkanbah. A DNW patrol report in August 1966 records:

> *The United Aborigines Mission appears to act as a transient depot for many natives. This was evident during Field Supervisors' visit to the Mission as I found natives who had walked off Christmas Creek and Cherrabun stations and were filling in time at the Mission. This was with the Superintendent's knowledge and consent. It was suggested to these people that they move on to other stations as much work was offering.*[7]

The same report, and subsequent correspondence, also dealt with issues raised by an increasing number of people camping near the hotel, in addition to the handful of hotel employees. The publican and his wife were agitating for their removal. The Licensing Court was suggesting the creation of a new reserve to accommodate these people. The DNW Commissioner wrote to the Chairman of the Licensing Court:

> *This Department does not have a native reserve in Fitzroy Crossing and it is felt that it would be unwise to establish and equip one at this stage. Experience elsewhere has shown that when such facilities are provided in pastoral country, they invariably attract*

a number of natives who would otherwise be employed on stations. Thus, an official native reserve in Fitzroy Crossing would probably result in a substantial increase in native population, many of them without satisfactory employment within the township.

The situation could easily change in the future of course, particularly if the union application now before the Commonwealth Conciliation and Arbitration Commission results in increased wages for natives employed on cattle stations. For this reason, the position will be watched closely and appropriate action taken as the need arises.[8]

It has been reported that equal wages were not implemented in the Kimberley until the early 1970s, after the Northern Territory. But a patrol report of a visit to Go Go in October 1968, just three months before the Christmas Creek mob were 'permanently discharged', seems to indicate otherwise. An assessment that echoes Tim Emanuel's views about an unwritten law, and is unusual for DNW in talking about traditional affiliations to land, also indicates that application of the new award is imminent:

As previous reports indicate GO-GO tends to be the 'yardstick' for other properties in the district. The natives are not ill-treated, neither are they particularly well treated, receiving only the basic requirements of sustenance and accommodation. Consequently less financially and/or less efficiently managed properties are not disturbed if their own particular standard of native welfare falls short of that existing at GO-GO, part of the influential Emmanuel [sic] Bros holdings. GO-GO lies on traditional tribal lands which the natives regard, quite properly, as their home. There exist few

> *ties to the GO-GO management, their loyalties being tribally orientated. This factor is of prime importance when viewing the significance of GO-GO's large native population.*
>
> *In the matter of the Pastoral Workers Award [name deleted, presumably the manager] advised, [name deleted, possibly Tim Emanuel] had advised the State Govt. that NO natives would be 'bushed' following implementation of the award on Dec 1st. Their policy would be to ration these station natives who remained during the 'wet'. Decisions on future employment would be made at the end of the wet when management would have sufficient indications as to workforce requirements.*[9]

In the same month there are patrol reports from Quanbun, Jubilee and Fossil Downs canvassing the issue. At Fossil Downs the patrol officer reported that:

> *The Owners have established a pattern of practical benevolence that is fast disappearing from the Kimberley scene. Conditions are not 'ideal' but natives are more than adequately fed and housed compared with the majority of local station conditions.* [Names deleted] *showed obvious concern about the implications of the Pastoral Workers Award.* [Name deleted] *advised that as many natives as possible would be retained although in several cases, men would by necessity have to be employed as 'slow worker'* [sic]. *It was made quite clear that no changes would be made until after the forthcoming 'Wet'.*[10]

At Quanbun Station, where they were still running sheep, he found:

> [Names deleted] *are strongly opposed to the forthcoming Pastoral Workers Award.* [Name deleted] *remarking that the natives were (quote) 'Far better off as they are' and 'are just not worth a whiteman's pay' (unquote).* [Name deleted] *believed that the Kimberley natives had not yet reached a stage where increased wages would be of any material benefit to them.*
>
> *From further discussions I gained the impression that management were in a quandary as how to cope with the implementations of the Award. Whilst completely opposed to native Unionism they were in a 'cleft stick' for, as* [name deleted] *remarked their shearers were strong unionists and it would only take (quote) 'one Redragger amongst them to cause all the trouble in the world'.*[11]
>
> *In contrast, at Quanbun's immediate neighbour, Jubilee Downs, 'The Manager stated that he hopes all the workers will become union members, however several of his male employees could only be retained on a "Slow Worker" basis and as such then wages would be subject to "negotiation" with the Union concerned.'*[12]

It is clear that as 1968 drew to a close, the Fitzroy Valley was in a state of tension, and of apprehension. Everyone knew that big changes were looming. It was not unlike the parallel build up to the wet season, feeling the temperatures rise, watching the clouds rolling in from the west, building and scattering, building and scattering, waiting for the first big storm. The storm arrived on 27 January, from an unexpected quarter, with the eviction of the Christmas Creek mob.

It is also abundantly clear that the Commonwealth Government had done absolutely nothing to make good on its undertaking at the time of the 1965 Equal Wages Case that 'If any problems of native welfare whether of employees or their dependents arise as a result of this decision [it] has made clear its intention to deal with them.'

The combined effects of the Conciliation and Arbitration Commission's 1965 decision, and the passage of the 1967 referendum granting Aboriginal people long overdue citizenship rights, that occurred during the transition period before the decision would take effect, meant that radical change in the pastoral regions of northern Australia was inevitable, and entirely foreseeable.

The inaction of the Commonwealth and State Governments in this three-year period, and the inadequacy of their response in the years that followed must be seen as ranking highly among the great policy and administration failures of Australian governments.

CHAPTER FOURTEEN LIKE A REFUGEE CAMP

At the Mission, oh it was quite shocking you know. The living conditions. I suppose you describe it as refugee camp you know.

Sort of people packed like sardines. Making little humpies. Hardly any room to move and there was a little space, a tiny little piece of land that you can all sort of pack yourself into and there only one toilet and one shower sort of thing. The conditions were quite poor.

Olive Knight

The Native Welfare file containing Acting Superintendent Kevin Johnson's handwritten notes about the eviction of the Christmas Creek mob is called 'Emergency Camp, Fitzroy Crossing', reflecting the sense of crisis in the Department. There is another handwritten note immediately after Johnson's first entries, even before Johnson's urgent telegram to the Christmas Creek Station manager less than a week into the crisis. This would suggest it must have been written almost immediately the camp was set up.

The note is from Sam Lee, also known as Chum Lee. He was a Lawman, and a stockman and drover of distinction, who had moved stock down the Canning Stock Route during the war. The rough cursive style of his note is formal, but to the point.

1. *All our young boys can get to work.*
2. *But old people can stay here.*
3. *I think we like to have a place.*
4. *We hoping not to get to far from here.*
5. *We would like to have nearby place.*

I must close now.

Sam Lee[1]

This is the first record of a land claim of any kind in the files. It is on file within a week of the first eviction.

Chum Lee was a Walmajarri man of gravity and substance. He would become one of the great leaders of the Fitzroy mob through the 1970s, and into the 1980s. But it would take him another ten years and many battles before he realised his dream of 'a place'. By 1979 most of the Christmas Creek mob had returned to live on an excision at Wangkatjunka, adjacent to the Christmas Creek homestead. But after a brawl involving the manager Kevin Norton—the same figure involved in the events of 1969—and a number of Aboriginal stockmen, Lee led another walk off, and founded the Ngumpan Community, adjacent to the Great Northern Highway, 90 kilometres from Fitzroy Crossing.

SND

Dear sir

(1) all our ~~yo~~ young boys can get to work

(2) But old peopel can stay here

(3) ~~A~~ I think we like to have a place.

(4) We hoping ~~not~~ to get to far from here.

(5) we ~~not~~ would like to have nears place.

I must close now

Samlee.

37

Sam (Chum) Lee's note to Native Welfare

There is no clear thread or pattern to the changes that overtook the Fitzroy Valley in the late 1960s and early 1970s. It was a period of turmoil and confusion; of rapid change, and few certainties.

Almost simultaneously with the eviction of the Christmas Creek people, there was a flare-up at Cherrabun Station. Head stockman and community leader Tarcoola Jugadan had an argument with the station manager. The details of the argument are lost in time, but not the aftermath. Tommy May was working there at the time:

> *'Come on.' That Tarcoola tell us, 'Come on. We go. We not live with this station. He can fix it himself. He can handle it by himself.' Horses and cattle and everything. Get all the young fellas and make a walk. Big walk. Whole lot. All the men. Only pensioners bin stay, and the women.*
>
> *We bin walk to that Ngalingkadji gate there. We came way down bush, in spinifex country, hiding away there. We bin thinking about that man he bin shoot him dead. Thinking about that.** *But we bin big mob.*
>
> *Next morning, we find tractor running across the road, from Go Go. This Jack Shaw, it might be Sandy Shaw, he bin give us a lift to Go Go Station.*
>
> *From there we bin go in another motor car, come to Fitzroy.*

---

* Tommy May says that there was a story, among the mob, that one of the managers at Cherrabun at the time had once shot and killed an Aboriginal man in the ranges south west of the station.

When the Cherrabun men reached Fitzroy Crossing, they found the Christmas Creek mob on the riverbank where they had been dumped by Kevin Norton. Tommy and the others joined the evacuation to the other side. As soon as roads and weather allowed, they organised for the Mission truck to collect the women and children and old people who had been left behind at the station. Harry Yungabun was one of the children:

> *Well I only a little boy then that time from Cherrabun and like I remember that old Mission, Bedford truck, come in there with old Uncle Jimmy Bieunderry and Charlie Rangi but they all gone now, they pass away. They come there to load up all the people in that time. In that time I didn't really understand. They bin take us to that Ngalingkadji Creek and Ngalingkadji Creek bin running too. It wet time. And they bin go back to get others from there and shift to old Mission.*
>
> *When I get to old Mission I still can remember all the old Bunuba people pointing out direction where they got to stop in each group. Like Walmajarri group that side, next to that cliff area; middle area all the Gooniyandi people for mix with Walmajarri from Noonkanbah, Quanbun side, Jubilee; and then that other end you go few people from Christmas Creek bin there and that middle row was mixed because some of the people bin already placed there in those little houses and family bin just mix up with them there, them mixed and like Bunuba, Nyikina people and Walmajarri people some of them and mixed, but this side of row, that middle part row where the road is it bin Wangkajunga people with all this Spider mob here they bin in that middle row with his brother there from David Down—all that family bin there in that middle*

row and other side where that, back to where that creek all the Bunuba, that's Bunuba land, people in there.

Yeah Bunuba bin like really good. Like sorting out where you camp somewhere. They sort you out like caravan park. Well that's how those people bin there now. But I bin reckon they do a good thing.

Some of the Walmajarri and Nyikina families who worked at Quanbun and Jubilee Downs stations, including the Bryants and the Thirkalls, had a 'holiday camp' over the wet season break. The camp was set up by a kurnangki, or fig tree, on high ground close to the emergency camp set up by the Christmas Creek mob. It seems that after the 1968/69 Wet they simply stayed on, never returning to work at the stations.

As a result, as the wet season receded and the 1969 mustering season approached, except for Noonkanbah, the swathe of cattle stations that formed the southern fringe of pastoral country where the Walmajarri people had settled were largely bare of their Indigenous workforce.

Within a year the Bunuba people left the stations where they had spent all their lives. George Brooking, who was a head stockman on the station where he was born, and from which he took his name, and Kevin Oscar, who would have been a teenager at the time, tell the story:

Kevin: When that changes came people had to move into town, I can remember. Kartiya bin say, 'Can't afford to have you, keep going.'

George Brooking

George: All Brooking and Leopold. What's that white fella at Leopold? All the people bin strike come to Brooking then. We come to Brooking. All mob. Nobody left there.

Kevin: When the place [Brooking Springs] was sold you see and the new managers bin come in, new owner bin come in, he bin look, look, look, like that, 'All you people off.'

George: We thought this bad bloke, when the new bloke came in. We was working for Bob Skuthorpe all our life, you know, and we didn't like to get away. We bin say, 'Oh we better leave too. Old boss gone,' we said and we walked.*

Kevin: I was on a motor car, we were on a little Land Rover moving into town from Brooking Springs. We were driving along. I can remember the kartiya pulled us up, the new station owner, Cameron Bell and all the Bell brothers, they pulled us up. Oh 'e bin find that crow bar there, pull that crow bar, 'That's not yours, that's from the station.'

'Nother lot of people walking along the river, walking all the dogs and cats and all the other gear, anyhow we were along the river.

We came in motor car then we jumped off, give all the old people to go on the motor car and we had to walk all them dogs and cats you know, on chain.

All the old people told us, 'Stay in the river, don't go outside on the

* Bob Skuthorpe, a long-term manager of Brooking Springs Station.

highway on the road. Stay in the river. Leave em all that dog and when you got leave them all the way along the river, don't come out on the highway.'

We went to Old Bridge and stayed there. All the way down to the old bridge and we started setting up camp there, where that Darlngunaya Community is now.[*]

Later on, two weeks later, Cameron Bell, he came back and he said, 'No I'm take all you people back.'

Some of them stayed up, some of them went back.

We bin there good while. Good while, when wet season and the flood came up, we still there. We used to get rations from Welfare.

The DNW files contain a report from the Shire of Derby West Kimberley's Health Inspector, dated February 1970, which includes a brief reference to this camp:

Camped on the Bank of the Fitzroy River in the vicinity of the A.I.M. Hospital, approximately a dozen families of natives are living in tents and rough bough structures.

There is no provision on this area for toilets, water, or rubbish.

RECOMMENDATION: The natives be removed from this area to appropriate reserve, or mission camp.[2]

---

* Bob Skuthorpe, a long-term manager of Brooking Springs Station.

And sure enough, they were removed, as Kevin tells:

> *The Welfare gave them little bit of land for family, blocks of land. The Mission bin giving all them. 'You, you take your family there. You, you take your family there.'*
>
> *He got wild Mr Smoker* [the UAM superintendent]. *'Go to all your little block ... it's enough to build a humpy. No more smoking, no more drinking, no more playing corroboree. You on Jesus ground now.'*
>
> *We bin get out of Brooking Springs. Yeah. I can remember it clearly. And we got pulled up along the highway there, along the road there. Oh biggest mob, Brooking family, Johnny Marr mob, all the Mission people mob.*

The Mission was bursting at the seams. Olive Knight recalls exactly what is was like living there at the time, compared to life as she had known it on the stations:

> [On] *the stations; well the conditions; well I suppose everything the facilities were there the same. Everything was same you know. But the thing is because of a huge crowd of people coming into a small space of land at the Mission that's what made it more appalling, you know, it was sort of like a refugee camp. More people packed in.*

> *Whereas at the station a lot more people spaced out and you did have an ablution block, well at least it's enough to service the number of people that were living on the station.*
>
> *The Walmajarri people were there. The Gooniyandi people were there and the Bunuba people were there. All were there. Together.*

When asked whether this crowding and mixing together of people created frictions or animosities between the different groups of newcomers, or between them and the Bunuba owners of the country, she is adamant that this was not the case:

> *No. I can't remember if there was any animosity there whatsoever because I think there was a sort of acceptance you know of the whole affair. A slow acceptance of it you know for people melding into the tribe and into intermarrying and all of that so when the intermarrying started happening it seemed that things, they couldn't move anyway. There was no room for hatred of one another or you know.*
>
> *I can recall there was no sadness ... people felt, 'Oh look we here now.' And we, they might as well make the most of it you know. That sort of thing and they felt quite fitted into the situation as it was, you know, and then they had to kind of adapt to what mission life was about and maybe find jobs in the Mission. A few of them did, a lot, you know, because they had to work a lot of those people too, at the mission. I think there was a lot of kind of settled feeling there you, know for that short, while till another lot of changes came along ...*

I can only remember the settled feeling in the Mission you know where everything was so kind of plain living and all that. It was like the station life you know, almost.

CHAPTER FIFTEEN NO GOING BACK

Well them old people ... they was there and they said, 'Well this country you know he's really Bunuba people and all bin mix you know. And they give them, 'Okay you can live there now.' We all bin living together.

Joe Brown

At the emergency camp the feeling was far less settled than the way Olive saw things at the UAM camp. There was not the existing structure and authority that the UAM exerted at the Mission. And for the authorities, the logistics of dealing with an emergency at remote Fitzroy Crossing were proving daunting.

Tents and tent-flies had to be flown up from Perth by DNW. Pit toilets were dug. Water was being carted daily from the UAM to the camp, but the old Mission truck was subject to breakdowns and the supply occasionally failed. Conditions remained appalling, and at times there were shortages of rations, with the two small stores at the Crossing Inn and the Mission not set up to cater for the numbers now living in the town.

No longer employed on the stations, the men were applying for unemployment benefits. The nearest office of the Commonwealth's Department of Social Security was 1,000 kilometres to the south in Port Hedland, and there were ongoing delays and difficulties in the processing of claims, leaving many families with no income for prolonged periods.

In early February of 1969 a list of 'Displaced Persons From Christmas Creek and Cherrabun Stations' totalled 213 people.[1] From this high point the numbers in the camp waxed and waned. Some people returned to both Christmas Creek and Cherrabun stations. Many of the top hands among the stockmen found work as waged employees on stations such as Leopold Downs and Myroodah, leaving their families behind in the camp.

The DNW files are full of reports on these movements; of attempts to classify the men according to their suitability and capacity for work; of reports and rumours from the stations of agitators and unrest and walk offs.

There is one reference to the reluctance of stations to employ men from the camp, which was seen as a hotbed of troublemakers. But equally, among many in the camp there was a determination to not return to the life they had left behind. Tommy May took jobs at Napier Downs and Myroodah, but refused to 'crawl back' when 'Managers oiling up, you know, [saying] "Come back work. Can you come back and work? I give you more money." Liar.'

A major report from the Kimberley Superintendent to the DNW Commissioner in June 1969 seeks to portray the situation as largely under control:

> *Investigations amongst most of the Pastoral leases on the northern boundary of the desert country in the Derby/Fitzroy Crossing districts reveals that there is no great displacement of pastoral*

> *workers as a result of the Pastoral Award. There is however, a considerable displacement of people, men, women and children (mostly family groups) caused not by retrenchment but rather a culling out by the stations of those people who are not considered an asset or even contribute to the function of the Pastoral industry.*
>
> *For the most part these people are those who over the past many years have wandered into these stations from the desert area ... They are very little removed from myall* or nomadic natives.*[2]

The report suggests that many of the men from the camp have found work and that there are only a limited number of totally dependent families at the Emergency Camp, and downplays or dismisses reports of further walk offs from four stations. It concludes with reports of an agitator in the district—reports which are never substantiated—and an attack on Jimmy Bieunderry:

> *I feel that people like Mr. James Biendarry [sic], who has been to Perth and met members of the Commonwealth Council of Aboriginal Affairs and has returned to Fitzroy Crossing and painted an extremely rosy picture of sweeping changes and a complete new deal for the aboriginal, has also contributed to confusion, disappointment and dissatisfaction when these changes have not become evident at an extremely fast rate.*[3]

Perhaps it is the wisdom of hindsight, but reading the files there is a sense of yesterday's men; bureaucrats of the old school of Native Welfare

---

* Bob Skuthorpe, a long-term manager of Brooking Springs Station.

protectionism; well intentioned, but trying to stop an inevitable tide. The outside world was finally starting to catch up with the Fitzroy Valley. Fitzroy Crossing was still very remote and isolated, but not totally cut off from the rest of the world in the way the stations were. Individuals like Jimmy Bieunderry were being exposed to new ideas and bringing them back to his people. But more than anything, there was an internal energy released by the changes that had overtaken the Valley.

The protectionists and welfarists had never got beyond seeing people as victims to one degree or another, and as units in the pastoral economy ranging from highly competent to 'myalls' needing 'culling'. Seeing the situation purely in terms of welfare, economics and employment, they failed to recognise the other fundamental changes that were happening.

Earlier chapters have described how throughout the pastoral era the people of the Fitzroy Valley held strong to law, language and culture. For all of the chaos and hardship of the fringe camps in these early years, this still held true. People may have been naïve and inexperienced in whitefella ways and politics, but their leaders were men of the law and men of the land. And they were hard men, tempered by bitter experience, and confident of their own knowledge and authority. After lifetimes of subservience they were now their own masters, however harsh their circumstances. They were more interested in building independent lives and new communities than contributing to the function of the Pastoral Industry.

By late 1969 the Department had acknowledged that at least some of the people were never going back to the stations, and that something had to be done about the situation in Fitzroy. The Emergency Camp was close to the bore and windmill that had been established for the public cattle yards that had been built ten years earlier; the same ones where Mervyn Street first saw cattle being placed on a truck. The authorities decided that this should be the site for a new camp with improved facilities including some basic housing.

Parallel to this official action, there was a discussion and negotiation happening among the Fitzroy mob, between the newcomers and the Bunuba traditional owners. Joe Brown recalls all the different mobs 'living together' on Bunuba country while Tommy May remembers the meetings and ceremonies involved:

> *That place, Windmill Reserve. That mob bin give us land. One old man* [from] *that Bunuba side. For Warrimbah. You know old Warrimbah, his Father.*
>
> *They give us the land, Mindi Rardi.* [There was] *a big meeting. But they had law here too; behind way.*
>
> *From Windmill side, back way, all that mob, they was sitting, tents there everywhere, waiting for house, Mindi Rardi.*
>
> *Some of them were the Bunuba side ... they bin all mix you know ... Johnny Marr was there. And that other old man, big tall fella, he from Junjuwa, I forget their names.*

The community originally known as Windmill Reserve, which would eventually become known as Mindi Rardi, was far from flash. The houses were of the old 'Type III' style, familiar on reserves around the state, and hardly deserving of the name; a tin roof, no ceilings, iron cladding that did not reach to ground level, and a trough on the verandah—just a slight step up from the corrugated tin shacks that had passed for housing on the stations. But it was the first sign of permanence in the new Fitzroy Crossing.

And while DNW was unaware of the fact, the new settlement was underwritten by a formal agreement between the Bunuba owners of the country and the Walmajarri and Wangkajunga newcomers, with Bunuba families such as the Marrs sharing residence with them, almost as if to demonstrate the reality of this.

The DNW had imagined that all the residents of the Emergency Camp would move the few hundred metres across to Windmill, but they did not reckon with the Kurnangki mob. In one of the DNW reports of 1969 they had been dismissed as interlopers at the Emergency Camp who had seemingly lobbed there by chance from Quanbun Station.

But Billy Bryant and his companions Wadgie Thirkall and Hairpin Marner were men of substance with opinions of their own, as Joe Brown recalls:

> *They moved this Wangkajunga mob over* [to the Windmill Reserve] *and this other old fellow now, Grandpa for this one there, he had that home in Kurnangki, he made that story. 'We are not going to move over there. We got to stay here.' They had to stay where the Kurnangki was.*
>
> *The old fellow* [Billy Bryant] *was well known you know when he had that community, he had to work in the pub to keep his*

community going. He had to keep that place going you know. And then he used to cart his own water from down pub way and this other mob that Mission used to still cart the water for this mob.

Billy Bryant and the Kurnangki mob were fiercely independent. Most of the other mobs dreamed of their home country, even as they struggled to find their way in the new world of the town. But the Kurnangki mob, with strong family ties to the Bunuba and Nyikina, seemed to have put down roots. Their camp of rough humpies was in many ways the spiritual heart and the intellectual centre of the new Fitzroy Crossing world. Tommy May describes the atmosphere there:

That old man, old Billy Bryant and his wife, they was really thinking hard. Meeting, every morning. You know. Sitting around and talking themselves and call the kartiya after.

That bloke was there too. Wombat [Williams]. *He was there too. What this, all this mob, his daughter and wife there. He was there. Poor fella. They was talking and properly strong, you know.*

Harry Yungabun, the youngster who left Cherrabun at the start of the walk offs in 1969, would go on to become a community bookkeeper, and eventually a senior worker at the Nindilingarri Cultural Health services, and a chairman of Marra Worra Worra. He was just a lad, but he remembers the time he spent at Kurnangki as fundamental to his development:

Well I bin like living like two way. I had my family still living at old Mission there, and I had my family, I found my new family in Kurnangki because my mum introduced me to all this

Thirkall family you know which I didn't know ... Since my mum introduced me to them, you know, and that's why I bin stick with them but I was still going back to my granny at, staying with my granny at, what you called the old Mission ... I just go like back and forward, you know ...

That's the 'nother old fellow my mum introduced me to, that's my uncle. Yeah. He was a Kurnangki boss. He was one of the traditional man, like Lawman you know. Leader, leader for every man, old people. After that when that old man bin pass away there at Kurnangki. That bin buried there in Kurnangki. That not too far from that last house. He was a traditional Lawman leader and then that uncle, old Billy Bryant bin take over and my mum introduced me to that old fellow again. And I reckon that old fellow really teach me, you know like culture side ...

I used to sit with him every night. Because my granny was there and I used to go and sit with him with my uncle there and teach me about like culture side. Respect. Talk to people.

It must have been the Kurnangki group, who always identified themselves as the Fig Tree mob, who erected the sign reading:

FIG TREE ABORIGINAL RESERVE
STOP AND LOOK
AND KEEP OUT OFF
THIS PRIVATE PROPERTY—2.2.70[4]

Hairpin Marner and Wadgie Thirkall outside Wadgie's home, Kurnangki, 1979

Harry Yungabun

Legally speaking the land was a Department of Native Welfare reserve, not private property, but the Kurnangki mob were unashamedly claiming ownership.

A year on from the first walk offs, it was clear that the town had permanently changed. The numbers at the Mission had exploded. The Fig Tree and Windmill camps were there to stay. The old township of just a pub, police station and post office was clearly a thing of the past.

But the authorities continued to try to corral and control events. The tone of the DNW report of February 1970 that records the Fig Tree sign is distinctly disapproving. In the same month there is the health inspector's report calling for the removal of the Bunuba families from their camp near the Old Crossing that leads to their removal to the 'Jesus ground' of the Mission.

A May 1970 report indicates a harder line developing from DNW:

> *There are a number of unemployed men on the reserve who have up to last week, been receiving Department of Native Welfare and Social Services relief. However, as from last week, all rations issues to able-bodied men were terminated, as local employment was offered to them, and none accepted the employment. Rations are now only being issued to deserted wives and genuine destitute cases, and it has been explained that this will not be extended to any unemployed men until the vacancies offered to them have been filled.*[5]

But the tide of events was continuing to run in the opposite direction. In August 1971 the last of the major walk offs occurred when the Noonkanbah mob left the station and came to Fitzroy. A DNW patrol officer's report records the events:

> *On Saturday 14th August an old woman ... had died. She had come from Derby a month previously, and had been sick then. There is currently an investigation taking place to determine if there were negligence, or callous indifference on the part of the Management ...*
>
> *There had been trouble brewing on this station for a long time due to the Management's attitude to the labour, and disputes over pay. About a week before the Inspection, the Manager's wife had sacked Domestic Biddy Ngidering for wasting water on the lawn sprinkler (she received her keep and clothes). Mickie Mick* [Mick Nicki] *organised the labour force to take the stand that if Biddy were sacked, they would all walk off. The Manager agreed and offered transport, but this was refused; two men set off to Fitzroy Crossing hoping to borrow the Mission lorry. They had not been seen since. On leaving the station the Inspecting Officer took aboard the Toyota one family. George Bell was met on the way in driving Billy Bryant's ramshackle lorry, and behind this in another rickety car came Friday Muller. By nightfall, the entire labour force had been evacuated.*[6]

When the Noonkanbah mob arrived in Fitzroy Crossing they established a new camp of their own, about a kilometre and a half from the Kurnangki camp at a place called Loanbung, on the high northern bank of the Fitzroy River.

CHAPTER SIXTEEN CAN YOU HELP US TO WORK ON OUR OWN

After the establishment of the Loanbung camp in 1971, there were only three cattle stations in the Fitzroy Valley with substantial populations that had stayed on. All three were in Gooniyandi country; the two elite stations of the West Kimberley, Go Go and Fossil Downs, and at the other end of the spectrum, Louisa Downs. Louisa went through a succession of new owners and managers, with conditions in the camp steadily deteriorating, but a community that hovered around sixty people stayed on there.

In Fitzroy Crossing there were now four substantial population centres: the Mission camp, and the squatter camps at Windmill, Kurnangki and Loanbung. They formed an arc around the two long-established hubs of the town, the Crossing Inn, and the cluster of the AIM hospital, post office and police station. The balance of the town had changed completely.

This would remain the basic shape of the town until two significant changes in the mid 1970s.

A new route was gazetted for the main highway, and construction began on the new all-weather bridge that would be well above the flood peaks of the wet seasons. One effect of this was to bring the three squatter camps into much more public view. Previously they had all been hidden away from the passing traffic; but now they all fronted the new highway route.

At the same time a new town site was gazetted, excised from Reserve 9656 which was the Mission reserve. Over the second half of the 1970s the old hospital and police station were closed down and relocated to the new town site, leaving only the post office in the old town centre. And housing began to spring up in the town site, primarily government houses for the gradually increasing number of public servants, but also a smattering of private residences. At the time this precinct was often called 'kartiya town' as there were no Aboriginal people there in the early years.

From the time people were displaced from their country, they were thinking of returning, and actively working towards this. One of the earliest and fullest and most poignant articulations of this comes in August 1969 in a DNW file opened in response to a query from the first federal Minister for Aboriginal Affairs, William Wentworth.[1]

Michael Angelo was a desert man, a Wangkajunga man; a quester and a traveller. Somehow in 1969 he had found his way to Sydney, where he left a letter with the Foundation for Aboriginal Affairs, who according to their letterhead were 'A Non-Political Non Sectarian Organisation Helping Aboriginal People To Help Themselves'. The Foundation was based in George Street in the city, and their secretary forwarded Michael Angelo's letter to Wentworth three days later with a covering note describing it as a 'very pathetic request'. The letter is roughly handwritten, but far from pathetic:

> *(Dictated by Michael Angelo) 18.8.69*
> *Can you help us to work on our own.*

Cattle
Make windmill
Make stockyard
Help make roads use tip truck
Make fences
Cart timber, use bulldozer
We want to live in a clean house (sick of living in tent)
We want money so we can buy clothes, food.
Only got little wages.
Own police boys.
White policeman growl too much.
They don't like us.
Want government to help us.
Maybe workshop, truck, landrover
Own property, own house.
Christian people want to live together, all family
Willing to work hard in Kimberley country.
Store, post office, office
Church, house, school and school teacher and house.
Hospital, native girls for teachers and nurses. Sports ground and equipment.
Who belong to West Australia?
Native? Who grow the cattle?
Native? Who grow the horse?
Native? Who grow the sheep?
Native? Who make the fences.
Native. Who make the yard.
Native

Michael Angelo
Tjantjuwa
Mission Church Fitzroy Crossing
Western Australia

In 1972, legislation from the new Labor government in Perth finally abolished the DNW after its forty-four year reign, replacing it with the Department of Community Welfare (DCW) and the Aboriginal Affairs Planning Authority (AAPA). Through the early 1970s the files of the new AAPA contain a series of approaches from Aboriginal people seeking land.

Early in 1972 Banjo Woorunmurra was 'making enquiries about Leopold and Fairfield Stations'. He attracts no support, with the file reporting that an anthropologist is 'of the opinion that the Bunuba people no longer exist as a homogenous or cohesive group, lacking in unity and leadership'.[2] It would take two-and-a-half decades, but this 'non-existent' group persevered, and in the 1990s the Bunuba Aboriginal Corporation was able to acquire first Leopold Downs and then Fairfield Station. In December of 2012, the Federal Court granted the Bunuba people exclusive possession native title over the two properties. To this day the Corporation is running a pastoral business, a school and community outstations on the properties.

In 1973 and again in 1974 Barney Barnes was seeking land at 'Pandanus Springs Noonkanbah area'. 'My father was born there all my family too,' he wrote. 'I can't go anywhere ... Please don't forget to reply.' There is no reply on the file.[3]

In 1974 Nipper Tabagee is requesting land on Kalyeeda Station, a request that would not bear fruit until decades later, long after the great man had passed away, when his grandson Ivan MacPhee was able to establish the Koorabye Community on land excised from Kalyeeda.[4]

In 1975 Archie Doherty writes a letter signed by himself and Norman Cox on behalf of the Louisa people, asking for a block of land on the Mary River to grow crops and vegetables, and offering to contribute towards the costs.[5]

The most persistent, dynamic and determined mob in relation to returning to country were the Noonkanbah mob at Loanbung. They lobbied endlessly, wrote letters, humbugged everyone they could think of. They tried a range of strategies and looked at all sorts of options, anything to establish a land base for themselves back in country. And in 1976 they were the first to succeed, when the Aboriginal Land Fund Commission purchased Noonkanbah and Millijidee stations, and they were able to return home as lessees, if not owners, of their country.[6]

All this activity was before the era of the Kimberley Land Council and the Marra Worra Worra Resource Centre, both established in 1978. There were no organisations or structures to represent people. The land claims and activism emerge through polite letters written by old men, through others written by sympathetic whitefellas who would relay the requests of men like Banjo, through dictations like Michael Angelo's, through representations to the Department of Community Welfare officers who had replaced the DNW men.

Revisionist historians and commentators have described the outstation movement as a misguided, socialist, utopian pipe dream driven by outsiders. But the truth is there in the records. From the very outset, the leaders of the 1960s and 1970s, who knew of Utopia only as a cattle station over in the Northern Territory, pursued the dream of returning to their country vigorously and relentlessly.

(157)

(Dictated by Michael Angelo) 15.8.69.

Can you help us to work on our own.

1. Cattle.

2. Make Windmill

3. Make Stock yard

Help make roads use tip truck.

4. make Fences.

5. Cart timber, use bull dozer

6. We want to live in a clean house (instead of living in tent)

We want money so we can buy clothes, food.

Only get little wages.

Michael Angelo's letter to Minister for Aboriginal Affairs, William Wentworth

2

own police boys.

white policeman growl too much

they don't like us.

Want Government to help us.

Maybe workshop, truck, landrover

own property, own house

Christian people want to live

together all a family

Jack Braeside, Michel Angelo

joint project (native boss)

willing to work hard In

Kimberley Country.

932/69

185 1

3

Store. post office office
Church, house. School, and
school teacher's house.
Hospital. native girls for teachers
and nurses. Sports ground
and equipment.
Who belong to West Australia?
native? who grow the cattle?
native? who grow the horse?
native? who grow the sheep?
native? who make the fences
native who make the yard
native.

MICHAEL ANGELO
TJANTJUWA
MISSION CHURCH
FITZROY CROSSING
WESTERN AUSTRALIA.

Apart from the success of the Noonkanbah mob, these dreams would not be realised until the 1980s and 1990s, but they were always at the heart of the mobs who found themselves in the Fitzroy Crossing fringe camps after the upheavals that began in 1969. But while they pursued these dreams, they also had to contend with the day-to-day reality of the fringe camps.

CHAPTER SEVENTEEN A POWER TO START FACING PEOPLE

It was a big shock to everybody, you know, people walking off, moving off from the station area to live in town. All I remember is living on the Mission there, the Mission at old camp, everybody just lived harmoniously, together, you know ... Lived in harmony. Good relationship with everybody all live together and they were no anything, no fights or anything like that. It was really good.

Topsy Chestnut

Fitzroy Crossing was still remote and isolated in the early to mid 1970s, to an extent almost unimaginable today. To those passing through, in transit or as visiting bureaucrats, it seemed like hell on earth. The fringe camps were right there on the main road where they couldn't be missed; squalid and overcrowded, rural slums reminiscent of the Third World.

The other element that could not be missed was the degradation and misery that revolved around the Crossing Inn. The binge-drinking culture of the white stockmen had been passed on to the men who got their citizenship rights, and from them to the mob at large. Moderate social drinking was never a concept that gained a foothold in Fitzroy and the towns of the north. Roughly once a year there would be a shock story in the *West Australian* about the horrors of life in Fitzroy Crossing.

There was a ferment of new ideas and activism and hope in the town, but this ran parallel to an orgy of self-destruction as rampant drinking and alcoholism quickly became a feature of life in the fringe camps. When people today look back at that time, they certainly remember the ravages of the grog.

Joe Brown sees it as people being overcome by the shock of the new:

> *From the '70s, you know, well that all the changes just come all of a sudden you know and we knew, 'Hello we bin getting, we allowed to drink the bar now.' We didn't have that sort of thing before and then coming free for the people to drink in the bar you know and that all sort of thing bin happen. Oh well you know, then we still never understand about this community life, how to live in a town.*

Olive Knight saw a gradual process of the drinking culture spreading its tentacles through the community:

> *Well people sort of embraced it* [citizenship rights] *with gladness more or less and said, 'Oh well, we'll just watch the Citizenship Rights people drinking.' They were sneaking in grog to some people but now it's made well good it's now open for everybody you know so it was sort of with open arms more or less they sort of received this news, the grog was now available to everyone. It started off that way then it became worse for a lot of us now where we didn't drink, the old people and all that, the grandmothers and all that.*

> *The women didn't drink at all. Only the men at first ... But they were into it with a force you know. They bin beating up their people and all that sort of thing and in the process draining themselves too.*
>
> *The younger men. Then it started going out to the older men and then to the women.*

Most of today's leaders went through it themselves; there are very few who at one stage or another of their lives did not succumb to the lure and the escape of the drinking life. One can only admire the strength and courage they exhibited in pulling themselves out of that world.

But while they certainly remember the negative impact of the grog and the damage it wrought, the appalling living conditions and squalor of the Mission camp and the fringe camps are not something that seem to linger in the memory today. Perhaps this is because it was in many ways just a continuation of what they had experienced in the station camps. In fact, many of the memories people have of that time are very positive, such as those of Topsy Chestnut:

> *They all lived real good. People didn't argue, anything, fight, or anything like that. Nothing. We didn't hear any, you know, people never even say, 'Oh why are so many people coming in here.' ... They had to just be together ...*
>
> *Just everybody in together because back in the seventies when people moved out from the station to go into town, people just came in anyway, you know. They just came in, they didn't, they didn't say, 'Oh this the Wankatjunka people.' Or, 'They's the Nyikina*

> *mob there.' You know. Or Gooniyandi, they just came in and, you know, accept these other people as if they were same people, all that, you know ... They just lived in harmony together in town, in Fitzroy.*

By 1974 it appears that the UAM was undergoing severe staffing and morale problems among its missionaries. An internal DCW memo says there is only one staff member left, and sees it as inevitable that the Mission will be handed back to the government. The officer indicates he has been approached by Jimmy Bieunderry—who by this time is in Carnarvon with Olive working as a Churches of Christ missionary—with a list of eleven men who are 'ready and waiting to run the mission'.[1]

The eleven named are a mixture of Bunuba, Walmajarri and Wangkajunga men who 'want this mission to be handed over to them by the government, to be run as a training centre and an aboriginal mission to be run entirely by aborigines'.[2] But a detailed report in September of that year concludes, 'To close the Mission at this stage would leave a vacuum that would be a disaster.'[3]

Another report in December, canvassing ways of keeping the Mission going, suggests that, 'If possible, approaches should be made to Mr. J. Bieunderry and his wife to return to Fitzroy from Carnarvon ... Mr. Bieunderry had considerable influence in Fitzroy as a diplomat and unifying leader before leaving for bible studies.'[4] It was only five years earlier that another officer of the Department had described Bieunderry as 'contributing to confusion, disappointment and dissatisfaction'.[5]

In the mid 1970s management of the hostels for schoolchildren was transferred to the DCW, and from about the same time people began moving from the old Mission camp as houses became available in the new village of Junjuwa, a kilometre down the road. The Mission survived as an institution, but its role and influence in the town shrank dramatically.

In the meantime, in October 1974 the State and Commonwealth Ministers with responsibility for Aboriginal Affairs, Norman Baxter and Jim Cavanagh, and their departmental heads, visited Fitzroy Crossing. They were simultaneously appalled by what they saw in the camps, and impressed by what they heard from the community leaders.

This visit would be the catalyst for a series of changes that would amount to a revolution in Fitzroy Crossing; a revolution that would have echoes throughout the Kimberley and beyond. By November DCW had talked one of their Wyndham staff, Stan Davey, into transferring to Fitzroy Crossing. Stan was no ordinary DCW district officer. He had a long history of activism in Aboriginal Affairs dating back to the 1950s in Victoria. When he first came to the Kimberley in the early 1970s he had a hostile relationship with the Department, and his work for the Department in Wyndham was controversial.

A memo from DCW Director Keith Maine in January of 1975 sets out Stan's brief:

> *The broad intention of Mr Davey's location at Fitzroy Crossing is to provide a specialist officer to work in close consultation with the local Aboriginal communities and our own staff so that we might assist in developing a programme aimed at maximum Aboriginal involvement in their own projects and affairs. For some time there have been moves made by Aboriginal individuals and groups at establishing economic projects and at returning to some of the near-by cattle stations ... Mr Davey should concentrate on what might be described as community*

> *development work with the Fitzroy Aboriginal population and not involve himself in other work normally undertaken by the District Officer.*[6]

Like the 'killing time' for the Jandamarra era, or 'dollar time' for the mid 1960s, 'Stan Davey time' has become a descriptor for an era among the Fitzroy mob. According to Harry Yungabun:

> *Well I reckon, it really should be to all the people they should thank Mr Davey. Stan Davey, they should really, just thank him for* [showing] *them how the kartiya thing work, you know, and where to go about, and teaching them how to face kartiya people. Not saying 'boss' and 'yes' and thing you know. He sort of like giving them a power to start facing people you know.*

CHAPTER EIGHTEEN REALLY STRONG LEADERS

They bin like form a group see and they bin saying like, 'We got to need to set up our own organisation.' You know, Walmajarri and Nyikina people the one bin set this thing called Marra Worra Worra, you know. And they say Marra Worra Worra, but it got three times. You got to say Marra Worra Worra Worra. Three times. That's how it used to be long time. Three times ...

Harry Yungabun

Stan Davey and his wife Jan hit the ground running at the beginning of 1975. Two white colleagues with similar attitudes were recruited, and locals Topsy Chestnut, Annette Kogolo, Kevin Smiler and Marty Stevens rounded out the team. They operated using a very particular model of community development that focused on enabling the community members to identify their own needs and goals, and empowering them to act on these in a concrete, step-by-step manner with defined, achievable outcomes.

This approach resonated perfectly with the people of the new Fitzroy

Crossing, who had left the old pastoral order behind, and were determined to build a new way of living, but had few skills and less experience in the ways of the modern world.

The energy and the ideas that had been building in those nightly discussions at the Fig Tree Camp and the other ramshackle new settlements now found voice and direction, and a clear way forward through these community development programs.

The second half of the 1970s was a remarkable period in the Fitzroy Valley, with a bewildering array of initiatives, and an unprecedented, transformative rate of change. The disparate mobs became incorporated communities. The Go Go mob became Bayulu Community. The Christmas Creek mob became Wangkatjunka Community. The disparate residents of the old Mission camp transformed into the Junjuwa Community. The Noonkanbah mob down at Loanbung incorporated as Kadjina Community, which in turn spawned the Yungngora Community. And Fig Tree Camp became Kurnangki Community. The Cherrabun mob had fractured somewhat, with people from that station finishing up at Kadjina, Junjuwa and Kurnangki, but a core group stayed together and became Djugerari Community.

Tim Emanuel became the first pastoralist in the Kimberley to make a serious attempt to come to terms with the new order. Negotiations led to the granting of one-square-mile excisions near to the homesteads on the three stations owned by the Emanuels, and plans were rapidly developed, and almost as quickly implemented for the establishment of new communities on these excisions.

At Go Go the people had never left the station camp, and there was a gradual and orderly shift from the camp to the new houses as they were completed at Bayulu, just over the hill. The Christmas Creek mob were able to return to Wangkatjunka, within sight of their old camp. It was the old-style humpies at first for most, but gradually the new village was built and people were able to move into whitefella style houses for the first time in their lives. Homemaker programs managed by Jan Davey generated new self-driven initiatives for women and kids, from school lunches to savings accounts for the whitegoods needed for their new homes.

The Mission mob were living on a reserve, so an excision process was not necessary. But a site called Junjuwa, on Forrest Road halfway between the Mission and the new town site, was selected for a new village. By 1978 the overcrowded camp that the Bunuba elders had run like a caravan park, according to Harry Yungabun's account, was no more as Junjuwa became the main single population centre in the spread-out township of Fitzroy Crossing.

In 1976 the determination and persistence of the Yungngora and Kadjina communities bore fruit, with Noonkanbah and Millijidee stations being acquired. These two mobs were able to return home, where they poured their energies into reviving almost derelict cattle operations and building new, truly independent communities. And in 1978, determined as they saw it to rescue their kids from continuing exile in Fitzroy Crossing, with help from Don Mcleod's Strelley mob, the Noonkanbah mob established the first independent school in the Kimberley.

There was an irrepressible sense of energy and excitement. It was indeed a new world that was being created.

And while each mob became a community, and pursued its own destiny, a common sense of purpose, and a cooperative spirit across the communities remained strong. The clearest expression of this was the evolution of Marra Worra Worra Aboriginal Corporation as a shared vehicle to support all of the new communities in their ongoing development. The recent Chairman of Marra Worra Worra, Harry Yungabun, has been involved with the organisation since its very beginnings when he worked as a bookkeeper as a teenager in 1976.

> *They had that old fella working with them, Stan Davey, you know, Stan Davey bin setting them up proper way before you start getting station or fighting government people, you got to have to set up your own organisation, office. So you can work from that office and once you start that thing you might start up 'nother mob station and thing, you know ...*
>
> *Well to me it's still happening. Like we recognise one town you see, all this group now what we bin split up now, we got ah, they saying four group in Fitzroy. You know Walmajarri, Bunuba, Kurnangki, Wankajunka, but they missing out Nyikina, Nyikina people here in town ...*
>
> *So it really not a four language group here, it's five language group. Five make Nyikina. Nyikina the one bin start up this Marra Worra Worra thing, Nyikina/Walmajarri bin start up and this other language group have come in ...*
>
> *Fitzroy, we recognise one town but all this language group. We work together. Mix up. And you don't see that sort of thing in another town. You don't see it and anything what we plan to do, we all get together. That's why this Marra Worra Worra thing is, resource is really strong for all the language group. And that's what happening now ...*
>
> *It go right back. Right back to that time. I can tell people like they*

want to ask me for that history like what I'm talking now for Marra Worra Worra, because people going to say, 'No you don't know nothing.' I think I been there with Marra Worra Worra from the day one ...

Me and Helen Malo was the first Aboriginal person to be recognised as a book-keeper to take the book out to the community, you know, to start up our own office. That's me and her now. And that's, I can still remember from that day when that Marra Worra Worra he bin start.

People might think, 'Oh this Marra Worra Worra started recently like any other resource centre in 'nother lot of town.' And this bin start a long time, them old people ... Strong old leaders. Even Bunuba you know. When I look at Bunuba I think back when these old people. They were really strong leaders and for all these all people here what bin lead us, Walmajarri people, you know, they were really strong leaders.

The official history on the Marra Worra Worra website[1] tells a similar story:

Marra Worra Worra is the oldest and largest Aboriginal Resource Agency in the Kimberley region of Western Australia. Its primary aim is to provide support services to existing and emerging groups in the Fitzroy River Valley, and to assist them to develop as strong, autonomous communities and organisations ...

Marra Worra Worra's other major role has been to act as a forum through which the Aboriginal people of the region discuss and act on issues of common concern. This is in fact how the organisation came into being in the late 1970s. At that time a community development program initiated by the State Department for Community Welfare was beginning the task of addressing the severe social problems that had arisen through a century of oppression and a decade of upheaval ...

The development programs were focused on the seven communities existing at that time. Leaders of these communities met regularly by a creek called Marra Worra Worra. By 1978 the meetings had become institutionalised under this name, and when the leaders decided to pool resources to employ a part time bookkeeper to provide basic financial services, it became an organisation with an office and staff. From this modest beginning, Marra Worra Worra has continued to provide financial services to member communities ...

The outstation movement, as it is often called, is the driving force of Aboriginal life around Fitzroy Crossing. This is reflected in the ever-increasing numbers of communities serviced by Marra Worra Worra over the years, from the original six, that became seven in 1978, twenty by 1984, and thirty-five by 1992. The process of small groups budding off from the large communities, seeking and eventually acquiring their own land, growing larger, and in turn spawning new groups is a dynamic phenomenon that still continues.

In that second half of the 1970s the strength and dynamism of the Fitzroy Valley communities became a model for others, and an inspiration throughout the Kimberley and beyond. However, two years after they returned home, the Noonkanbah mob found their precious new independence and freedom threatened by a wave of explorers chasing diamonds and oil. When the American oil company Amax announced they were planning to drill on sacred land not five kilometres from the community's base at the old homestead, they refused to bow to the seemingly inevitable.

The two-year struggle of the Noonkanbah mob to defend their land against Amax and the State Government went to extraordinary lengths. Their cause acted as a lightning rod that galvanised first the Aboriginal people of the Kimberley, and eventually the nation. It became an international cause celebre, and the launching pad for the Kimberley Land Council to become a significant voice for the Indigenous people of the region.[2]

And as the official Marra Worra Worra account suggests, the communities of the Fitzroy Valley continued to grow and evolve, and continued to work together.

CHAPTER NINETEEN A FAMILY TOWN

From the 23 'natives' listed by the Department of Native Welfare as living in Fitzroy Crossing in 1965, the numbers in the town have grown to approximately 1,000 today, including the major communities of Junjuwa and Kurnangki, the smaller communities at Darlngunaya and Mindi Rardi, and those in the town site and other spots within the town boundary.*

Fitzroy Crossing has grown and spread. Only in the wet season, when the clusters of buildings can be seen to be the only islands rising above the spreading floodwaters of the Fitzroy River, does its geography make sense to an outsider. But the foundations for the revolutionary changes that have occurred in Fitzroy Crossing had been laid long before Stan Davey and his colleagues arrived in town. The town had its genesis in a remarkable generation of men and women who had endured the worst of the station era, and survived to become the leaders and the inspirational force for the invention of a new world.

Fitzroy Crossing thus became a unique and special place. Most of

* A 2009 study (Population, People and Place: The Fitzroy Valley Population Project, Frances Morphy, Centre for Aboriginal Economic Policy Research, Australian National University) counted the Indigenous population of the town at 942. The commonly used figures are a population of 1,500 in the town area, with estimates that approximately 70 per cent of this number is Indigenous, with a further 2,000 Indigenous people living in the outlying communities of the Fitzroy Valley.

the major Indigenous population centres of the north, like Bidyadanga and Kalumburu in the Kimberley, and Wadeye and the Arnhem Land communities of the Northern Territory, are isolated reserves. Fitzroy is an open town on the main highway, where the Aboriginal majority is comfortable and confident. Through cooperative action they have been able to build a community that is 'their town' in a way that so many other towns of the Kimberley and the rest of northern Australia are not.

After the first wave of change in the late '70s and early '80s, Fitzroy Crossing again led the way with the establishment of a network of community organisations and Indigenous-owned businesses that dominate the commercial and social life of the town. Each of these has found a way of incorporating the inclusive model of the 1970s whereby all the diverse communities of the Valley and all the language groups are incorporated into the governance structures.

But Fitzroy Crossing is so much more than this. It is a place where the mob works together, and feels comfortable. As Harry Yungabun explains:

> *People* [should] *look not only the negative side, they got to look at the positive side too now. What's happening here in town. Fitzroy is different. If they come down here and spent time they would see it is different. Like people have their business and like this office Nindilingarri, like we got partnership with the hospital.** *In other town they got no partnership, they working separate, and we starting to build up partnership with each organisation you know. Like Marra Worra Worra, Karayili, KALACC, got a KLC there and Marninwarnti Resource Centre. And when anything happen, like we all get together. We share our thing, resource to community people and we bring community in ...*

* Nindilingarri Cultural Health Services, where Harry Yungabun works.

> *All I can just say is people need to work together like what they've done before* [when] *all the language group was put together at the old Mission. They not bin separate or kicked out or anything and from there I reckon this thing is, I reckon that's why they just make people in Fitzroy being together and even though we got community outside, all around now where we stopping separate but to me I know Fitzroy people, we all together in one ...*

Harry uses exactly the same words as Olive Knight:

> *This town is a family town ... It's different. You can see people sitting on that park there, near the Tourist Bureau, they feel comfortable. You can sit down near that supermarket outside, they feel comfortable. No looking over their shoulder. 'Oh look im, this bloke bin growl me because I'm sitting down here.' You can walk into the shop. Any shop around here in Fitzroy. You don't feel that nervous ...*
>
> *Any place around here you won't feel nervous. Even that footy oval. You look at that footy oval. You don't have the gate locked.* [It's] *open all the time. Kids just go in there and play all the time, not feeling nervous or; you can go there this afternoon, maybe sit down and have a rest. You can go sleep there. You got no fear. Haven't got people coming and waking you, 'This not a sleeping area.' You know.*

June Davis and Mervyn Street express similar sentiments:

> *June: We feel at home there.*

Mervyn: Everybody come here.

June: Because I don't go shopping [in] *Halls Creek. Oh we bin go Broome and come straight back, Derby, but in Fitzroy you can take your time, all day you can stay there, you know. You've got places to go and sit down and relax and talk to people. You've got friends and families in there. You come back here and your own community and people like to go back into town they can stay and come back, and go straight back again.*

Mervyn: We mix in there. We mix in. Kartiya and blackfeller we mix in in Fitzroy. Everybody in Fitzroy.

June: It's like a home. Fitzroy.

Mervyn: Still home. Like we got a place there.

June: It draws people from all over the place.

There are thirty-five distinct communities in the Fitzroy Valley, from Jimbalakudanj, 120 kilometres west of the town, to Yiyili, 170 kilometres to the east. The people draw their heritage from five different language groups: Bunuba, Walmajarri, Gooniyandi, Wangkajunga and Nyikina. The communities and the individuals who live in them are different each from the other in many, many ways. But they also feel a strong bond of common interest and solidarity as 'the Fitzroy mob'.

This is a legacy of the men and women of the 1960s and 1970s who had the courage, the wisdom and the foresight to be friends and partners in dire times; to help each other and to make life better for each other rather than build fences.

Fitzroy Crossing as it exists today is a town born out of trauma and dispossession and hard times. It is still struggling with that legacy. But it is also a remarkable place with a remarkable story.

As Olive Knight says:

> *That strong bond remains from the past. It didn't change. It's still there. Grog didn't take it away you know. It's still there. Running right through us.*

ACKNOWLEDGEMENTS

The financial support that made the field work, research and writing of this book possible came from the Fitzroy Futures Fund and the Community Histories program of Lotterywest. Thanks to the Governing Committee of the Fitzroy Futures Forum for their decision to approve this as a 'Lighthouse Project,' and to Lee Grmas at Lotterywest for her patience when it seemed it might never be finished.

Many people assisted along the way. Annette Kogolo was a huge help in organising the first round of field work in 2008. Anneli Knight also assisted with notes and transcripts of the group sessions. Kathryn Thorburn assisted with the early research, and working out the shape of the project. Wes Morris and the Kimberley Aboriginal Law and Cultural Centre were always helpful in keeping it on the rails. To Kaye McLennan and Laurel Smith, many thanks for the work transcribing all those interviews. Bill Bunbury pointed the way to help fill some gaps in the research. Alex Mountford came to the rescue, and did a wonderful job with the portraits of the storytellers. Michael Gallagher kindly supplied some of his photographs from 1979–80, and Paul Elliott supplied the photographs of Mervyn Street's beautiful mural. Janet Hutchison has been a delight to work with as an editor.

Material from Mangkaja Arts has been used in the biographies of Tommy May and Mervyn Street, and from *Out of the Desert* in the biography of Olive Knight. David Berteaux created the original schematic map of the communities of the Fitzroy Valley that has been adapted here.

I thank all of the storytellers for their contribution, their time and the cuppas. And I thank Joe Ross for getting the whole thing started.

ENDNOTES

CHAPTER ONE

1. SRO Series 2030 1944/0972; Native Matters—Fitzroy Crossing.
2. Western Australian Statistical Register 1965–66, Part VI, Factory Statistics, p. 77.
3. SRO Series 2030 1944/0972; Native Matters—Fitzroy Crossing.
4. Ibid.
5. *The Daily News, 4/11/1950, in SRO Series 2030 1949/0263; Fitzroy Crossing. Establishment of a native Institution at.*
6. SRO Series 2030 1952/0372; Fitzroy Crossing Native Depot. Handover to United Aborigines Mission.
7. SRO Series 2030 1952 /0485; United Aborigines Mission. Fitzroy Crossing. Rationing of Natives and subsidy.
8. SRO Series 2030 1961/0144; Fitzroy Crossing Mission. Register of Inmates.
9. SRO Series 46 NDG 23/10/4; Missions, UAM Fitzroy Crossing—Reports Annual & Patrol.
10. Ibid.

CHAPTER TWO

1. Mary Durack, *Kings in Grass Castles*, Lloyd O'Neil Pty Ltd, 1974, p. 329.
2. For a full account of the Jandamarra story see *Jandamarra and the Bunuba Resistance*, Howard Pedersen and Banjo Woorunmurra, Magabala Books, 1995.

CHAPTER THREE

1. Steve Hawke & Michael Gallagher, *Noonkanbah: Whose Land, Whose Law?*, Fremantle Arts Centre Press, 1989, p. 66.
2. Ibid, p. 66.
3. Ibid, pp. 51–52.
4. Peter Biskup, *Not Slaves Not Citizens*, University of Queensland Press, St Lucia, Queensland, 1973, pp. 24–25.
5. DNW file 1930/0300, *Native Matters—Leopold Downs*, per Department of Child Protection.
6. Constable 1665 to Chief Protector Aborigines, July 1936, in 1930/0300, op cit.
7. Ibid.
8. Ibid.
9. Constable 1665 to Chief Protector Aborigines, 7 September 1936, in 1930/0300, op cit.
10. Ibid.
11. SRO Series 2030 1944/0972; Native Matters—Fitzroy Crossing, memo dated 7/12/45.
12. *Noonkanbah,* op cit, p. 65.

CHAPTER FOUR

1. *Noonkanbah*, op cit, p. 56.
2. *Out of the Desert: Stories from the Walmajarri Exodus*, Magabala Books, Broome, Western Australia, 2002.

3. Ibid, pp. 1–2.
4. *Noonkanbah*, op cit, pp. 58–59.
5. 'Captured!' English translation, in *Out of the Desert,* op cit, pp. 125–35.
6. Letter dated 13/5/1942 in SRO Series 2030 1930/0308; Native Matters—Christmas Creek Station.
7. SRO Series 2030 1930/0308; Native Matters—Christmas Creek Station.
8. Ibid.
9. Ibid, memo dated 14/7/1942.
10. Ibid.
11. Ibid, Constable to Commissioner of Native Affairs, 11/9/1942.
12. Ibid, Commissioner of Native Affairs to Constable, 21/10/1942.
13. Ibid, Constable to Commissioner of Native Affairs, 19/9/1942.
14. Ibid, various memos and correspondence.
15. Ibid, Sergeant to Commissioner, 2/8/46.
16. *Out of the Desert,* op cit, pp. 62–69, includes a story from Limerick, *'An adventure with camels'*, about his travels through the desert with two Afghan cameleers, when he was still a boy.

CHAPTER FIVE

1. SRO Series 2030 1930/0308; Native Matters—Christmas Creek Station. Letter dated 12/01/1939.
2. Ibid. Letter dated 28/11/1939.
3. SRO Series 2030 1938/0746; Margaret Downs Station or Go Go Station.
4. SRO Series 2030 1938/0752; Native Matters—Brooking Creek Station.

CHAPTER SIX

1. See *How The West Was Lost,* Don McLeod, 1984.
2. SRO Series 2030 1944/0972; Native Matters—Fitzroy Crossing.
3. Ibid.
4. The *West Australian,* 24/6/1950, in SRO Series 2030 1949/0430; West Kimberley District—Native Matters Generally.
5. Ibid.
6. SRO Series 2030 1949/0456; West Kimberley District Officer, Derby, Patrol Reports.
7. Biskup, op cit, p. 241.
8. SRO Series 2030 1949/0456; op cit.
9. Ibid.
10. Ibid, Patrol Report No. 1–49/50, 9/8/1949.
11. Ibid, Patrol Report No. 2–49/50, 13/9/49.
12. Ibid. Patrol Report No. 62–49/50, 29/11/49.
13. Ibid.
14. Western Australian Statistical Register 1965–66, Part VI, Factory Statistics, p. 77.
15. SRO Series 46 NDG 36/045; Stations: Louisa Downs via Derby.

CHAPTER SEVEN

1. SRO Series 2030 1950/0719; West Kimberley District. Patrol Reports; Patrol Report No. 4–50/51, dated 11/9/1950.

2. SRO Series 2030 1938/0746; Margaret Downs Station or Go Go Station; Welfare Inspector to District Welfare Officer, 14/9/1961.
3. *Out of the Desert*, op cit.

CHAPTER EIGHT

1. SRO Series 2030 1951/0422; Fitzroy Crossing Native Depot. Register of Inmates.
2. SRO Series 46 NDG 38/011; Fitzroy Crossing.
3. Kimberley Language Resource Centre, *Moola Bulla: In The Shadow of the Mountain*, Magabala Books, Broome, 1996.
4. Ibid, pp. 184–88.
5. *How The West Was Lost*, Don McLeod, 1984, pp. 89–93.
6. SRO Series 2030 1953/0129; Northern District Office (Derby). Journal.

CHAPTER NINE

1. SRO Series 2030 1938/0749. Native Matters—Louisa Downs Station.

CHAPTER TEN

1. SRO Series 46 NDG 23/10/4; Missions, UAM Fitzroy Crossing—Reports Annual & Patrol.
2. Ibid.
3. Ibid.
4. Ibid.
5. Ibid.
6. Ibid.
7. SRO Series 46 NDG 29/07; Schedule of Pensioners —UAM Fitzroy Crossing.
8. Interviewed by Bill Bunbury; quoted in *It's Not The Money It's The Land*, Bill Bunbury, Fremantle Arts Centre Press, 2002, p. 120.
9. SRO Series 2030 1966/0016. Summary of Station Report Survey 1963–1965.
10. DNW file 1947/0735; Noonkanbah Station—Employment—Living and General conditions—Reports and statistics re, per Dept of Child Protection.
11. SRO Series 46 NDG 36/045; Stations: Louisa Downs via Derby.
12. SRO Series 46 NDG 36/009; Stations: Bohemia.
13. SRO Series 2030 1938/0752; Brooking Creek Station.
14. SRO Series 2030 1961/0144; Fitzroy Crossing Mission. Register of Inmates.
15. SRO Series 46 NDG 36/045; Stations: Louisa Downs via Derby.
16. Western Australian Statistical Register 1965–66, Part VI, Factory Statistics, p. 77.
17. Ibid.
18. DNW file 1947/0742; Margaret Downs Station —Employment, Living and General conditions—Reports and Statistics re (also known as Go Go Station), per Dept of Child Protection.

CHAPTER ELEVEN

1. SRO Series 2030 1966/0016; Summary of Station Report Survey 1963–1965.
2. SRO Series 46 NDG 36/045; Louisa Downs via Derby.
3. DNW file 1930/0300; Native Matters—Leopold Downs, per Dept of Child Protection.
4. SRO Series 2030 1938/0749; Native Matters—Louisa Downs Station.

5. DNW file 1947/0735; Noonkanbah Station—Employment—Living and General conditions—Reports and statistics re, per Dept of Child Protection.
6. DNW file 1947/0742; Margaret Downs Station—Employment, Living and General conditions—Reports and Statistics re (also known as Go Go station), per Dept of Child Protection.
7. Ibid.
8. Ibid.
9. Ibid.
10. Ibid.

CHAPTER TWELVE

1. SRO Series 46 NDG 31/02/4; Emergency Camp; Fitzroy Crossing—Reserve No. 9656.
2. Ibid.
3. Ibid.
4. Ibid.
5. Ibid.
6. Ibid.
7. Ibid.
8. Ibid.
9. Interviewed by Bill Bunbury; quoted in *It's Not The Money It's The Land*, Bill Bunbury, Fremantle Arts Centre Press, 2002, p. 120.

CHAPTER THIRTEEN

1. For a fuller account of the Equal Wages Case, see Bunbury, op cit, and *Equal Wages for Aborigines: The Background to Industrial Discrimination in the Northern Territory of Australia*, Frank Stevens, Aura Press, Sydney, 1968.
2. Interviewed by Bill Bunbury; quoted in *It's Not The Money It's The Land*, op cit, pp.×88–89.
3. Commission ruling quoted in Bunbury, op cit, p. 69.
4. Ibid.
5. SRO Series 46 NDG 31/02/4; Emergency Camp; Fitzroy Crossing—Reserve No. 9656.
6. DNW file 1947/0735; Noonkanbah Station—Employment—Living and General conditions—Reports and statistics re, per Dept of Child Protection.
7. SRO Series 2030 1944/0972; Native Matters—Fitzroy Crossing.
8. Ibid.
9. DNW file 1947/0742; Margaret Downs Station —Employment, Living and General conditions—Reports and Statistics re (also known as Go Go station), per Dept of Child Protection.
10. DNW file 1949/0736; Fossil Downs Station—Employment, Living and General conditions—Reports and Statistics re -, per Dept of Child Protection.
11. DNW file 1947/0744; Quanbun Station—Employment, Living and General conditions—Reports and Statistics re-, per Dept of Child Protection.
12. DNW file 1947/0743; Jubilee and Nerrima Stations—Employment, and Living General conditions—Reports and Statistics re -, per Dept of Child Protection.

CHAPTER FOURTEEN

1. SRO Series 46 NDG 31/02/4; Emergency Camp; Fitzroy Crossing—Reserve No. 9656.
2. SRO Series 2030 1969/0791; Fitzroy Crossing—Aboriginal Matters (1968–74).

CHAPTER FIFTEEN

1. SRO Series 46 NDG 31/02/4; Emergency Camp; Fitzroy Crossing—Reserve No. 9656.
2. Ibid.
3. Ibid.
4. Ibid.
5. Ibid.
6. DNW file 1947/0735; Noonkanbah Station—Employment—Living and General conditions—Reports and statistics re, per Dept of Child Protection.

CHAPTER SIXTEEN

1. SRO Series 2030 1969/0932; Michael Angelo—Aboriginal Enterprise Financial Assistance (1969–73).
2. SRO Series 2030 1972/0381; Fig Tree Reserve—Community Project—Fitzroy Crossing (1972–73).
3. SRO Series 1779 1974/0600; Aboriginal Land Rights Claims—Barney Burns [sic]—Pandanus Springs—Noonkanbah area.
4. SRO Series 1779 1974/0602; Kooroobye Aboriginal Assoc.
5. SRO Series 1779 1975/0208; Application for Land—Archie Doherty & Norman Cox.
6. The full story of this struggle is told in Noonkanbah, Fremantle Arts Centre Press, 1989.

CHAPTER SEVENTEEN

1. SRO Series 46 NDG 18/2; Organisations, Associations & Societies—Aboriginal Housing Society—UAM Fitzroy.
2. Ibid.
3. Ibid.
4. SRO Series 1099 A4090 V1; Localities and Districts—Fitzroy Crossing District Matters—General Correspondence; 19/9/74-10/12/75
5. SRO Series 46 NDG 31/02/4; Emergency Camp; Fitzroy Crossing—Reserve No. 9656.
6. SRO Series 1099 A4090 V1; Localities and Districts—Fitzroy Crossing District Matters—General Correspondence; 19/9/74—10/12/75.

CHAPTER EIGHTEEN

1. http://www.marraworraworra.com.au/about.
2. The full story of this struggle is told in *Noonkanbah*, Fremantle Arts Centre Press, 1989.

ABBREVIATIONS:

AAPA: Aboriginal Affairs Planning Authority
DCW: Department of Community Welfare
DNW: Department of Native Welfare
KALACC: Kimberley Aboriginal Law and Cultural Centre
UAM: United Aboriginal Missions

PICTURE CREDITS

Front cover (top) & endpapers: Relief Mural painted by Mervyn Street with technical support from Craig Snell, Tarunda Supermarket Fitzroy Crossing 2004; destroyed by fire in 2009. Mural images courtesy of Mangkaja Arts Resource Agency, photo collage by Paul Elliot
Front cover (bottom): Landgate
Back cover: Alex Mountford
Line drawing (internals): Patricia Mamajun Torres
Frontmatter: p6 Adapted from Paul Marshall; p7 David Berteaux
Chapter one: p26 Guy Hayes, Mangkaja Arts; p30 State Records Office, File 2030 1952/0485
Chapter three: p41 Michael Gallagher
Chapter four: p50 Michael Gallagher; p55 State Records Office, File 2030 1930/0308
Chapter five: p61 State Records Office, File 2030 1938/0746; p64 Alex Mountford
Chapter six: p71 State Records Office, File 2030 1949/0456
Chapter seven: p76–77 Relief Mural painted by Mervyn Street with technical support from Craig Snell. Mural images courtesy of Mangkaja Arts Resource Agency, photo collage by Paul Elliot; p81 Alex Mountford; p85 Alex Mountford; p87 Alex Mountford; p89 Alex Mountford
Chapter eight: p95 State Records Office, File 2030 1952/0383; p99 Alex Mountford
Chapter nine: p105 Alex Mountford; p107 Alex Mountford
Chapter ten: p116 State Records Office, File S46 NDG 29/07
Chapter eleven: p129 Alex Mountford; p131 Alex Mountford; p133 Alex Mountford
Chapter twelve: p139 Alex Mountford; p142 Michael Gallagher; p143 Alex Mountford; p146 State Records Office, File 46 NDG 31/02/4
Chapter fourteen: p158 State Records Office, File 46 NDG 31/02/4; p163 Alex Mountford
Chapter fifteen: p173 Michael Gallagher; p174 Alex Mountford
Chapter sixteen: p182–84 State Records Office, File 2030 1969/0932
Endmatter: (author) p211 Alex Mountford

Steve Hawke grew up in Melbourne but found his way to the Northern Territory and then to the Kimberley, in the far north of Western Australia, as a nineteen-year-old in 1978. Captivated by the country, the history and the people, he stayed for almost fifteen years working for Aboriginal communities and organisations. He now lives in the hills outside Perth, but continues his strong association with the Kimberley, returning most years. His writings on the Kimberley include Noonkanbah: Whose Land, Whose Law? (1989), Barefoot Kids (2007), a children's novel set in Broome, and the play Jandamarra that premiered at the Perth International Arts Festival in 2008, and toured the Kimberley in 2011.